A FEW SMALL DETAILS

# A FEW SMALL DETAILS

Essays on Design and Other Excursions

**Steve Diskin**

Cover: Viaduct, Ljubljana-Maribor, Slovenia
7: Camel Market in Kwara Tigi, Niger, West Africa
16: Stairway at the Church in the Barje, Ljubljana, Slovenia
28: Big Ear, national satellite earth station, Leuk, Switzerland
36: Potsdammer Platz, Berlin, Germany
48: Helix Clock (photo: Richard Clark)
56: Portrait of Irena Praznik
61: Kurent at the festival in Ptui, Slovenia
62: Baltic Sea, Tallinn, Estonia
68: Grape arbor in Osor, Croatia
76: Snowy A2, Ljubljana, Slovenia
80: Highway reststop, France
86: Kunsthaus, Graz, Austria
94: Fireglass
98: Hagia Sofia, Istanbul, Turkey
102: Stairway, Vltava River, Prague, Czech Republic
113: Cat, Los Angeles
114: Poet and Dragon, montage
122: Clouds
127: Chair 13, National and University Library, Ljubljana, Slovenia
128: Headless author, Ljubljana, Slovenia
Author photo by Diana Pau

# TABLE OF CONTENTS

| | |
|---|---|
| *Africa on My Mind* | 7 |
| *A Few Small Details* | 17 |
| *The Fly on the Ceiling* | 29 |
| *In the End There Was the Word* | 37 |
| *Sentimental Mass Production* | 49 |
| *Fear* | 57 |
| *Antarctica* | 63 |
| *An Evident Kiss* | 69 |
| *A Short Riff on Mobility* | 77 |
| *And What About Industrial Design?* | 81 |
| *For Forty Years I Have Tried to Understand the Moon* | 87 |
| *Toast in One-Syllable Words for Tim Butte* | 95 |
| *Ode to an Earn or Hey!* | 99 |
| *Inside* | 103 |
| *Two Loves at First Sight* | 109 |
| *A Message in a Bottle* | 115 |
| *An Argument Against Cheap* | 123 |
| *Off With His Head!* | 129 |

# AFRICA ON MY MIND

On the globe, connected now by satellites and the great emerging neural network at geographical scale, for anyone who calls himself a designer, especially those who teach, and for explorers of the world of design, its creative process, its meaning, a trip outside of oneself reveals how easy it is to become trapped in a fixed mindset and familiar rules. It is the right moment to make friends with the rest of the world. Take a trip to Africa.

The sun rises slowly over Niamey, the capital of Niger, shyly shrouding itself in the steel gray mist which hovers over the red earth until midmorning. It is a poem recited over and over everyday, much as it is in the rest of the world, but here with a special quality that is so strong and so deliberate that it seems to warp time and space. It was thus in other places and other times, notably five hundred years ago in the waning days of the Middle Ages, when a particular construct of the universe formed another set of ideas, aesthetic, social and spiritual, temporal and spatial in Europe. On any morning in Niamey you can be sure that when the sun does finally burn through the sky and when suddenly it is too hot to think, that the character of the Middle Ages is alive, if not well, in Africa.

Niamey is best approached from the "real" world by airplane, traversing 2500 miles of blackness to an oasis of light. Your flight departs from Paris at midnight; the route is due south. The Cross of Agadez sparkles in the eastern sky, your only point of reference in the blackness, much as it is still for nomads in the Sahara. In Africa however, it may be more intriguing, if one were able, to arrive in Niamey by camel, overland, leaving the vibrating edge of the advancing desert for the relative fecundity of the Sahel, the savanna where acacias grow and where, especially in the morning, there is time to sit and think about where you are.

You have come here to meet your brethren on the global network, but on this turnoff from the highway, that which appears virtual is real nonetheless. Against the background of a digital magic carpet, the flesh and blood of the people you will meet shatters disbelief. At the airport in Niamey, at five AM, where you are greeted by sweet air and the smell of smoke hovering in the black atmosphere, there is a great bird on the tarmac, a vehicle of airborne nomads, industrial designers and bearers of news, ambassadors of time and space who descend into a strange land in the stillness of early morning.

This bird is fast; fifteen minutes after landing, it has disgorged its cargo of souls, flapped its aluminum wings and disappeared, swallowed by the sky.

Acquaint yourselves with new friends in the airport, some in military dress, others in colorful robes, or muted cotton clothing congenial to a hot climate. You are offered assistance by hundreds of hands, you are engulfed by a gel of human molecules, a culture thick with immediacy and smoldering. A white Mercedes takes you through the emerging metallic morning haze to a hotel where exhaustion transports you to another realm of fitful sleep, regeneration, enculturation, a shifting like the Sahara, where the grains of sand are your brain cells looking for some stability, for a home. You awaken a different organism, the clothes in your suitcase look alien. Are these strange hands really yours? A camel lopes across the boulevard in front of the Ministry of Uranium. This is life as usual at 13° N. latitude, due south of Greenwich.

Shake hands with the Hausa, Djerma, Fulani and Tuareg, as you walk down the street past the marketplace where products of a strange land are bought and sold, as you cleave through another gel of time and space, remembering how things used to be in the so-called "real" world. In a surprising instant you hear the sound of a distant viola da gamba and inhale one last 500-year-old breath of the Middle Ages. And here you realize, relieved in a way, yet also with trepidation, that the twenty-first century enters not in a measured procession of kings and queens, but tensely, in a swirling dance on five-and-a-half billion little pairs of feet.

Welcome to the New World.

An age of perceptual innocence is coming to an end. Here for the last time you can see the world through medieval eyes, when objects seem to burn with spatial incandescence on a landscape of clay and sand, far away from the modern labyrinthine megalopolis with ins and outs of steel, granite and multiple vanishing points. Here, you see things differently, naively and beautifully. Granaries, twisted trees, huts, a mosque, a cloud: these objects are mysterious, isolated and wonderful; they defy explanation. Here it is possible to believe that the earth is flat. Here, people and houses huddle together not only for warmth and companionship, but also for art, making a composition of form on the horizontal plane, making sense of the three-dimensional world. It was thus in the Middle Ages before linear perspective, that moment of spatial truth, the gift the Renaissance would later give to painting and the representation of space on a plane.

> *Central perspective...was a dangerous moment in human history. The new principle did away with the creative freedom of both perception and representation. Perspective is... a mechanical print traced on a pane of glass... a given view of the object at a given moment took the place of the totality of experiences, accumulated during a lifetime. In central perspective... infinity appears at the very center of tangible space.(3)*

In Africa, infinity is quite noticeably everywhere, and your clock is the sky and the stars.

This is Niger, home to 7,000,000 people, 90% of whom live within 100 km of the southern border, in the grasslands surrounding the capital. Niamey is growing rapidly and so is the incidence of crime. It is not much different from the rest of Africa in this regard. Ethiopia is 3000 miles to the east. It is there that the Leakeys found Lucy, the ancestor, the mother. Now, on this continent, malaria, AIDS, and river blindness are shaping the new society. Here in Niger, an 83-year-old blind chief is ostracized, his elegance and power consumed by aggressive microfilariae carried by black flies. Poverty and drought have driven the population to the cities. Is Africa, the human birthplace, also a model for demise, the disappearance of a world we once knew?

> *...some lived in tiny cabins of crossed lath stuffed with grass or straw, inadequately shielded from rain and wind. They lacked even a chimney; smoke from the...fire left through a hole in the thatched roof... Folklore was rich in violent tales, for death was their constant companion.*

> *Life expectancy was brief; half the people in Europe died, usually from disease, before reaching their thirtieth birthday... Travel was slow, expensive, uncomfortable and perilous...bridges spanning rivers were shaky; the roads were deplorable – mostly trails and muddy ruts...(2)*

As the Middle Ages waned, so now does Africa wane. Disease has become an icon, a manifestation of a deep current, a sadness below the surface. It is a sadness known in the Middle Ages.

> *O miserable and very sad life... we suffer from warfare, death and famine; cold and heat, day and night, sap our strength; fleas, mites, and so much other vermin make war upon us... Life is very short. (1)*

> *Of the approximately 12 million people worldwide who are HIV positive, 8 million are in Africa.... But it is malaria that is most responsible for the disease wall that threatens to separate Africa and other parts of the Third World from more developed regions of the planet... It is mutating into increasingly deadly forms... resistant to current... antidotes. (4)*

Blinded Africans are talking about destroyed lives, begging in the capital city to feed families in the bush. Where are the mighty Tuareg now, once the great warriors of the desert, to protect against invisible hordes? Alas, knives of brass and iron in scabbards of leather and ebony are useless against the invaders of the future.

It was a Wednesday morning, traveling in Land Cruisers, crossing the

John F. Kennedy bridge which spans the Niger River, passing camels and rusty trucks, beggars, galvanized steel shacks, a suburban mosque, twisted trees, men and women walking in surprisingly large numbers along the main road. A businessman dressed in a flowing bubu, carrying a briefcase, strides purposefully towards Niamey. What this man would not do for a bicycle. This is an industrious, if widely distributed, population zooming into the twenty-first century directly from the Middle Ages without the 500-year breathing space of Renaissance, Industrial Revolution, and quiet cultural doldrums in which to think and plan.

We are standing under an acacia, out of the hot sun, hearing the murmuring in French of a team of doctors, powerbooks in hand, who are charting the spread of river blindness. Here, high-tech medicine meets the Middle Ages. Chaos cries out for understanding.

Much as the sun now blazes across the horizontal plane of West Africa, so too did light fall on the gloom and calamity of medieval Europe, as the collective perceptions of man came to illuminate the landscape.

*...Pessimism is the ground whence (men)...will soar up to the aspiration of beauty and serenity. For at all times the vision of the sublime life has haunted the souls of men, and the gloomier the present is, the more strongly this aspiration will make itself felt.(1)*

In the early 1400's, let's say on a certain day, the knowledge of linear perspective produced a rite of passage. The medieval mind had probed for answers and found myth, spirituality and formality. In this world, dragons breathed flames, heroic knights and distressed damsels alike came to terms with space and time. A small population, scattered here and there by whatever destiny, thinned by plague or famine, wrestled with identity on the "x-y" plane.

To make a friendly space, humans began to populate the world with buildings and products: cathedrals, to attract space like a magnet and organize it along visible lines of force; and objects, books, jewelry, musical instruments and weapons, with which to give ritualized meaning to the world. Craft led to the celebration of the work of man – in short, to the Renaissance.

> *The rediscovery of Aristotelian learning and the full cultural heritage of the Greeks and Romans began to reappear...In the long reach of history, the most influential Renaissance men were the writers, scholars and philosophers; however, their impact wouldn't be felt until later. The artists began to arrive first, lead by the greatest galaxy of painters, sculptors and architects ever known. (2)*

The final coup was the Industrial Revolution: a manifestation of central perspective, a world controlled by science and art, and mathematical exactitude. Now, after 500 years, facing a second industrial revolution, a subatomic, cerebral and cyberspatial one, man, looking for shelter and having exhausted the obvious possibilities, creates electronic communication, a huddling together for digital warmth. Curiously however, if this is a second industrial revolution, then it has preceded a second renaissance where thought and art could infuse this revolution with meaning. For the first time in history solutions precede their own problems. Technology has outpaced need, and humans now sit in playpens full of toys, wondering what they are all really for.

This is an embarrassment of riches of the highest order imaginable, and perhaps a reason why hunger and violence, real and metaphorical, now also characterize the social environments of rich Western cities. Can we really dare to call Africa primitive? Something is wrong. This ghastly estrangement from life represents a hunger both primitive and unsatiated. Sadness and violence, calamity and indigence, famine? Even now?

Five hundred years from the exuberance and discovery of a first cultural awakening in Europe, there are once again broken civilizations throughout the world.

The tools of the Renaissance, the paint brush, the pen, the viol, the human voice and the block of stone produced a fusion of form and material, of process and aesthetic. Brain and hand fused to make things of beauty, treasured objects, artifacts of communication, if you like.

And now the rules have changed, as the perspective of time and space has changed. The medieval town is now the urban sprawl, with:

> ...*rapid population growth, inadequate health care, and environmental scarcity, chaos and violence...Tyranny is nothing new in West Africa, but it is now part and parcel of an increasing lawlessness that is... a natural point of departure (for) what the political character of our planet is likely to be in the twenty-first century...To see the twenty-first century truly, one's eyes must learn a different set of aesthetics. One must reject the overly stylized images of travel magazines... there are far too many millions whose dreams are more vulgar, more real – whose raw energies and desires will overwhelm the visions of the elites, remaking the future into something frighteningly new... The past is dead...(4)*

In all great cycles of life on Earth, poverty and sorrow give way to great hope and achievement. For every medieval age there will someday come a renaissance, and likewise all beacons of light which penetrate darkness will themselves at some point be extinguished. In a way, it is all a matter of point of view.

Certainly with the gyrations which produce the future will come another spatial and temporal renaissance, in which what we now fear will come to be seen as OK: a new perspective, shall we say. Alberti and Brunelleschi, givers of vanishing points and receding planes, were to the first Renaissance what Negroponte and Spielberg are to the second, if we can call the digital age a second Renaissance, and arguably it is. Within decades the inevitable future "space" will take care to make the reality of whatever gloomy situation seem much brighter. The pain of great change will only last a little while.

I see a vast space under a sky with black clouds. A horizon, bonco cylinders with thatched cone hats, a twisted, expressive baobab tree, a market place, bulbous water vessels, the river, the figures of Leonardo, Descartes, Piero della Francesca, Giotto: they have come here to visit Oumarou (one of Niger's leaders), Doctor Soga (head of the river blindness program), Raya Loutou (a young architect with her own design office in Niamey) and Ibrahim (a 10 year-old boy in Kware Tigi), to sit and discuss the meaning of time and space. The plans we make are a timeless striving for the divine and a battle against the ponderous force of gravity which would bind our aspirations to the ground. At this great gathering, students of design are asking probing questions for which their professors have only tentative answers. Recession has prompted queries like "How will I ever get a job?" But lately, at the waning of an amazing century, students ask "What's it all for?"

The answer goes like this: It is Friday in the camel market at Kware Tigi, the poorest outlying suburb of Niamey. If objects define a space, this space is extraordinarily thick with definition: among huge piles of straw mats and iron fences painted green, camels walk like great robotic machines, out of scale. Walls made of rusted, twisted automobile sheet metal enclose the environment. Thinking about the rise and fall of Lucy, standing on the land, watching a strikingly beautiful human figure swathed in fabrics of colorful wildly-clashing patterns, carrying a jar of water on her head along the horizon, feeling time pass rather slowly, you begin to see hope in the fiery incandescence of the sun. Yes, it's true that you can also see Africa's fragmenting social structures, waning traditions, declining quality of life and craft, even the threat that what makes this land beautiful will be destroyed.

> *For at all times the vision of the sublime life has haunted the souls of men, and the gloomier the present is, the more strongly this aspiration will make itself felt. (1)*

Fruit bats still fly overhead at dusk. A blue heron descends onto a spit of land in the river. Antelope horses gallop across the bush. Animals populate the landscape of Africa, anchoring its space to living, moving objects, anchoring its existence in infinite time. The human race was born in this land and as long as people everywhere in the world are making music, talking to each other, using their imaginations, and taking a good look around, there is some hope.

As we speak, your African friends are sitting around laughing and telling stories over a bright green Diablo cocktail of mint and soda. Come through the courtyard of bougainvilleas to Raya Loutou's office and see the future Niger on the drawing board. The stars still flicker over Niamey at night, the moon still casts its reflections on cool, beautiful rice fields. The granaries are full for now and stand resplendent on the infinite horizon, while the people who care about the destiny of this country and the world are hard at work to make it better.

You just have to smile when you stand at the edge of a craggy outcropping of rock at La Tapoa, one of the unique topographic features of southwestern Niger, in Parc W, where the river enters the country at the border of Burkina Faso, in early morning, watching a family of baboons play and then, all of a sudden, sit and face the rising sun. Elephants trumpet sound into the air. It's the music of time, a poem of space. Free at last. In this joyous moment, you can't help but think...it's all for this.

*[Narration for video Africa on My Mind presented at the IDSA National Design Educators Conference, Detroit, 1994 - text published in the proceedings of the conference]*

1. *The Waning of the Middle Ages*, Johan Huizinga
2. *A World Lit by Fire: The Medieval Mind and the Renaissance*, William Manchester
3. *Art and Visual Perception*, Rudolf Arnheim
4. *The Coming Anarchy*, Robert D. Kaplan, in *Atlantic Monthly*

# A FEW SMALL DETAILS

In the ecology of the designed world, there is a deep symbiosis: for each object created, there is a recipient of that creation who becomes, in effect, an archivist in a personal museum of the details of civilization that are being built every day. The artist, the critic, the collector of insects, architect and inhabitant, designer and consumer, the machinist and the hobbyist are among the participants in an ecology of design, along with observers whose hungry eyes and brains catalog and celebrate the evolution of creativity.

This was my first thought while falling asleep one night, when I saw myself in a white room in a white bed, on the way to the world of dreams. Rainbows of rich detail of the days events flashed overhead as my brain sifted through the staggering array of quotidian bits, coming to terms with the information of life on Earth.

The brain at night is an active organ. It murmurs the passwords of the world of dreams, as it discovers and arranges those words in its untamed dictionary from among the details which reside in the minds of the inhabitants of the Earthly globe. The brain is at work whether its human host is asleep or awake. It's one bit in the matrix of details that constitutes a life.

> *Digital eyes open and close. It is very late here; most people are falling asleep around you, while somewhere on the other side of the world people are awaking, walking, playing music and sailing in ships.*

The globe of details never sleeps. As the hypnogogic state gives way to sleep I see fire, a tantalizing blaze of chemistry and physics, a violent change of state.

This fire restores form, this chaotic dance fuses molecular elements into shapes. The flames unfold their meaning soon. I see my own shoes. Now I can walk in this dream.

It is the first step forward of a journey into a world of details, a digital world now composed of zeroes and ones, constructed from the flames of our collective imagination. Here, there are only details; here, there are no details at all.

People pass by and you understand them just by looking at their shoes. Shoes are museums of the minute features of design; people value these details and display them proudly: material, style, size and shape, and color. At first glance shoes may all seem pretty much the same, but this world of shoes, a few small details in the vast chronicle of human invention, if left to expand in the vacuum of space, could indeed become a small galaxy, a tapestry of variations like a magic carpet.

It is a story about ingredients. If cooking is about the selection of certain tasty materials, processed by some rule or other, by morphing at a the molecular level by heat or chemistry, or macroscopically by beating, cutting and stirring, then design is the tasty application of some aesthetic process or intuition to a variety of materials, by morphing macroscopically or at a level of what we might call "detail". Taste an exotic stew and you will know everything about design.

At the interface of darkness and light, of air and water, this delicious broth, boiling and steaming, has a surface like the great ocean – a typhoon excites wind and waves. Beneath this surface, however, is a different world, the global unconscious, the ingredients of dreams.

We are all human, but our apparent sameness is an average of the innumerable parameters of physiological and perceptual detail. A measure of the fine detail of human personality is manifest in choices. If you are what you eat, then you are also what you drive, how you live and how you look. The sum of all choices is a definition of human character. You are what you choose.

Bellbottom pants rise as a fashion phœnix from 25-year-old cultural ashes, and you wonder to yourself how anybody could have liked these? Proportions, angles and materials, resident in automobiles, chairs and pants, are part of the real stuff of design, the daily ingestion of minutiae which apparently have great meaning. But like a perfume that gradually fades in intensity after a first breath, it must also be that a similar process of saturation occurs visually, gradually making people immune to some details as they get mesmerized by others. Or maybe it is more that no product can really be considered apart from the environment in which it exists, as sensation blends into a background of sense ingredients that you can't see, smell or taste very clearly anymore.

*She is as beautiful as the molecules which follow her. She is an interface, a boundary layer of sight, smell, sound and sensation, mathematics and particles of light. This is real perfume.*

Clothing oneself is the process of taking care of details, for without details in clothing, there would be no notion of appropriateness, allure, power and ceremony.

And more than clothing, the human body itself is the apotheosis of detail. At Yale, in 1954, William Sheldon tried to make a lexicon of the variations in human form. In the Atlas of Men, he correlated the details of height, weight and shape, relating the numerous body types to the characteristics of animals. This was nothing less than the bringing of the mythology of the stars to the earth, making us wonder yet again who we are and what we allow ourselves to see.

Nature is, if nothing else, a thesaurus of detail. Look at the microgestures in the human face which can communicate universes of meaning. This is more than corporeal astrology to be sure. It is nothing less than a matrix of how to read the human character.

*It is more than I can comprehend, from flaming shoes to naked men, from a face to the heavens. I must be dreaming. Associating freely I arrive at another intriguing interface, of humans and tiny chemical machines.*

Homeopathy, brainchild of Samuel Hahnemann in the late 1700s, offers a tantalizing medicinal postulate that a poison which can cause a symptom can cure it as well. Hahnemann ingested minute quantities of quinine and got the symptoms of malaria. He experimented with all kinds of compounds and logged the effects; the research he started has continued for over 200 years in many countries in the world.

Substances recorded in homeopathic texts include a truly bizarre assortment, among which are extracts of jellyfish, lava, bees, mistletoe, petroleum, gunpowder, tarantula, lead, antimony, skunk, stork bill, plaster and turpentine!

There are over 2000 so-called "remedies" that have been studied and their effects on humans documented. These now constitute a great book with over 459,000 details in more than 9,000 categories. And whereas there now exists two centuries-worth of research, it requires a sensitive practitioner to know how to apply it, and an intelligent patient, conversant in the tiny, even esoteric, details of his own bodily function. You must watch carefully for symptoms like irritability in the open air, trembling internally when playing the piano, pain in the head from wet feet, ecstasy on walking in the moonlight!

> *She spins and spins in a glorious spiral beneath the moon, dreaming wildly and reveling in the light of the orb. A trumpet sounds a dance of ecstasy, a gyration, a tribute to the heavens.*

Homeopathic medicine was one of the precursors of the digital age, a hint from 200 years ago about the future of details and the fading image of what we like to call "the big picture". A remedy works or it doesn't. Little molecular switches toggle back and forth signaling "yes" or "no".

In chemistry, an ion moves, an electron appears and suddenly your microscopic universe becomes an entirely different place. It can kill you. Or save you.

If chemistry seems very far from the things that usually concern us, then how about micromachines? Drink a glass of little routers and your arteries are cleared? Add a handful of microbrushes to a bucket of paint and relax while your fence gets a fresh coat of pigment? (It may take a couple of years!) This is all about details and note that everywhere we turn, our designer sense is being focused downward to infinitesimal levels, smaller than we ever thought. Miniaturization seemed benign, but we are beyond that former stage into the totally deconstructed realm of bits.

Here, matter equals information. This is where virtual reality lives. Here, every detail is a clue, but what exactly is the mystery? There is water on the surface of the Earth and in the roots of the plants which grow outside the window, but there is water somewhere else, in dreams, where a ship can sail on the land. The detail as we know it has ceased to exist. Good-bye, old friend!

The landscape of the world is strewn with details, bits of information, seeds in a universal garden, remedies and poisons in vials inside the global medicine cabinet. People who say that you have to look at the big picture ignore the fact that the digital world is nothing but detail. Almost all objects from buildings to cars, from toasters to tiny articles of jewelry can be reduced to sameness or magnified to differentiation from other similar things by the scale of your point of view. A car does not know that it is a car. Does it?

So let's go for a drive. It is irksome to think of all cars as being identical; but they are. Why else would manufacturers have to put name tags on their sheet metal babies so that you can tell them apart? For the enthusiast in a car culture, however, the details speak about sex, power, speed, beauty – a smile, a sneer, winking, breathing, snarling. All of this talk from a 4-wheeled box. But for the people who design and make things, the detail is God.

It is supremely human to be interested in this little bit or that, despite the other human need to philosophize on a grand scale. An analog world, with big pictures and small details, implies hierarchy – that is, one feature of a thing being more important than another. But in the world of information and VR, there is a very interesting consequence that all particles large and small join in a single conceptual community of being. It is an analog person who looks at things in relative importance. It was a nice world while it lasted, but now it's gone. Soon you will begin to see the world only as a matrix of bits, themselves in other matrices of digital realities, and all of them are "virtual" except one. But which one? Never before has reality been so confused, and so exciting! One bit, one primitive information unit from another recipe and you're in the twilight zone. The devil, as we all must have suspected, is in the details!

Some people say that you can't have a thought without language. Poets look to the dictionary when they need a word. Physicists ask mathematicians.

If the new world is truly digital, then there must be a mathematical representation for it: an algorithm. Let's invent a thing, call it T. It's just a list of characteristics, and we decide how long the list is. Designers modify the details of a thing: changing the structure of its information. And let's say that civilization is the sum of all things designed. No bit can escape the designer's hand of change. Bellbottoms are back and suddenly we are left wondering if there is a god, or a devil, in the details or any other place!

Let's play with this. Here's a person, say its your best friend: with nanotechnological precision, change a biomechanical detail and you have a have a naked friend, maybe with a stainless steel head. Alter another parameter and your friend has a fish for a heart.

We have now quantified the whole universe and it's flawless. The universe is now the sum of its parts, and you can make a complete catalogue of those parts. This is sometimes called the story of the "universal library". Here's how it goes...

You have 26 letters, capitals and lower case, some numbers and punctuation. Say it's 100 characters all together. You decide to write every book in the English language. The math is simple: just a few details, like lines per page, characters per line and voilà: your library has $10^{2,000,000}$ books. Forgetting that the combinations are more numerous than the atoms in the entire galaxy, you assign the problem to your computer and some billion years later you have it: every book ever written, every book now being written and every book that will ever be written. Most are unreadable. Some are pretty wild, like Moby Dick, but this time it is by Ralph Melville. We start with the great white whale, but then you have great white giraffes, cars, CD players, and houses. And now consider design, symbols and icons, parts, fasteners, sub-assemblies, materials and packages of those materials and the variety of forms, functions, semantics, marketing, and manufacturing in a universal warehouse. And the variety of tastes and ingredients, spices and herbs in the universal goulash yet to be created by you, tonight, from the offerings of the universal supermarket!

Oh boy, I can taste it now, as I realize that just at the moment we think we have discovered everything, do we realize that we are just beginning. We have found the algorithm, though, and it is nothing more than the street address of the universal library...

Designers sift the universe for its most promising ingredients, comb the indices of the books in the universal library for its richest details. Here there is a map of Denmark, but all of the cities are have Chinese names. There is a collection of the musical scores of Johann Sebastian Bach transcribed for a chorus of bagpipes and leaf blowers, and a directory of all of the designers in France, but all of their phone numbers ring in a phone booth in the lobby of a small hotel in Mexico City. Here is the novel Lolita by William Shakespeare plus trillions and trillions of encyclopædias with totally wrong information, almanacs where the moon never rises, and catalogues of all of the clothes you have ever worn, captioned by all the phrases you have ever spoken, photos of every device you have designed and sketches you have made. You are the author of every book ever written. And that's true of every other person in the universe, real or imagined, living or dead. This is graffiti on the largest scale imaginable.

On a certain day, the space shuttle Challenger blew up... some little detail about the O-rings. A 747 strays into foreign airspace. Computers make errors. A gas tank in an old truck catches fire. Detail is not only a matter of a nice radius, a parting line, a texture or color, when a poor choice of a material can contaminate a river. Homelessness, carjacking, rain forests, pollution and AIDS: someone must once have said they were minor details in the great scheme of things. The real story of disease, and of good fortune as well, originates at the molecular level and is developed in the details of what we see and do. Look at this planet and you can see the chaos originating in small events.

The lowly millionth decimal place does make a difference. Weather forecasters found that out, along with people who theorize about the length of the coastline of Great Britain. The so-called "details" of its ins and outs, bays and peninsulas, craggy outcroppings and white cliffs matter very much. Just ask a fish and a bird to compare their calculations.

We are designers. Our love of details and the fact that our names are already written on all the chronicles of design deeds large and small, makes us in some way the guardians of the future. If you accept this idea that god is in the millionth decimal place (you know, the story that a butterfly flapping its wings in one place brings rain to another place far away), then you really also have to agree that there is no telling what the results of our work might be. Let's flap our designer wings in New York, Paris, Los Angeles and Copenhagen. Who knows? The sun may then shine a little brighter, if chaotically, in New Delhi, Capetown, Moscow and Antarctica.

Consider the game of tennis. Like DNA, a tennis ball in flight carries a code, including one which says whether the shot will be in or out, before it hits the ground! Winning often occurs at a thin white-painted boundary; the difference between in and out is a digital bit. Each stroke of the racquet is the sum of the details of angle, velocity and position. And more than that, the racquet also imparts to the ball a revelation. In or Out. Yes or No.

It has been claimed that there were once 30,000 languages on the globe, but now there are 5,000. What is happening here? Like the tennis ball's genetic code, so does a language have a code, including a bit that foretells extinction. By the way, all objects of design have this bit, too. Languages have complex visual messages, important to graphic designers or cryptographers. Palindromes and sentence reversals, at the interface of "design" and "word" are particularly interesting linguistic details. Language, like homeopathy and industrial design, is a dynamic matrix of tiny tennis balls of information that invites you to come out and play.

As physicists search for the grand unification theory, poking around in the lower depths of sub-subatomic particles, designers, in the meantime, are confronting our own deconstructed world of pointillist fragments. As a consequence, there's less and less difference between an object and its environment. It's just a change in information density defining an edge between what's in and what's out. Like tennis. What's "in "and "out" also characterizes a styling fad, and if there's any definition of styling, it's the small changes in detail looked at against a frozen moment in cultural time, a snapshot of the background environment. Evidently we are unable to be very objective about stylistic detail because the immediate visual foreground is very dynamic and clear while the environment is always slightly out of focus. But one thing we know is that foreground and background are always changing into each other. Bellbottoms are here; does this mean that fins on cars are not far behind? The small bit in a flying tennis ball that prophesies its future inhabits the minds and bodies of humans, their civilization, their clothing and automobiles.

I see the angle of a certain pant leg, wondering: "now I must wear this?" When an object changes form, the entire environment around it changes. Flared pants live comfortably in a flared world – an object drags its environment along with it when it moves. This is a design theory of relativity. As the object goes, so goes an entire nation tied to it by invisible strings. Like marionettes and puppeteers. There are certain connections here. No wonder a certain material causes cancer. No wonder in the '60s we thought everything was so beautiful. Object and environment are the same! In light of this I proclaim: the detail is dead! Long live the detail!

There is a saying in Japanese which goes: *Matsu ni matsu no kaze; umi ni umi no kaze.* For a pine tree, a pine tree wind; for the ocean an ocean wind.

Things are changing and I recognize the impossibility of separating object and background. A design "dream boat" must sail in water, not on the drawing board.

Imagine: A small boat sails away from the shore to worlds of nature unexplored that far exceed the constructs in the minds of man in complexity, richness and meaning. As the shore disappears over the horizon it is possible that the way back to this world will be lost.

In 1 AD, the perfect digital year, Ovid wrote: "In all creation no thing endures, all is in endless flux, each wandering shape a pilgrim passing by... what was before, is left behind; what never was, is now..."

Was this really day one of the digital world, two thousand years ago? Did object and environment get stuck together forever in 1 AD? And can designers ask that question with any hope of finding a transcendent object?

Look at all the things you admire and sometimes you find a serene, timeless quality in your favorite ones. But now, in a digital commercial world, we call certain objects classic, even when they have only been around for a few years. Where is real transcendence to be found, and would we know it when we see it? Are there objects which are not destined for extinction as prophesied by their digital DNA? Classical music, nature, the human form, geometry? Is time itself the only truly transcendent construct of man? Or can we really find truth and beauty in a fine pair of shoes?

Shoes? I am back where I started. What was once solid transforms into fire, into vapor, into air. There is no doubt I am waking up from a dream. In the morning, every molecule is in action. Coffee perks, toast browns, the radio blares the news, electrons surge through copper pathways, the atmosphere is alive with broadcast. The new carpet outgasses its adhesive aromas. The kitchen cabinets puff plumes of formaldehyde while innocent packets of poisons once resident in medicine cabinets ride little streams of impure water through pipes into a network that doesn't even stop when it arrives at the sea, but continues further, deep into the ground and far into the air, to be eaten or breathed. Bacteria multiply by the billion on the head of one bristle in a toothbrush, while green plants and colorful flowers whisper to each other in the living room.

While you were asleep your brain organized gigabytes of information, and satisfied with its work, it reflected to itself, "Ah, this is good", and for fun, ran through some dreamy film clips from archives of memory forgotten until now. Elsewhere, guilt racked your conscience, self-doubt gnawed at your ego. Waves of alpha rhythms crashed on a beach.

The ability to recognize minute detail is one of the fundamental components of survival of the species on the planet, from bats capable of locating their babies' voices inside a cave of thousands of screaming offspring to a man detecting passion, or a lie, in a momentary twitch of a tiny muscle in the soft facial skin near his lover's eye. We humans, as for all beings and all things, are unique packets of information in a quantum universe, which the tools of the electronic age have brought into focus. A universe of bits. Where does it lead? To global digital democracy and a richness of expression hitherto unknown or a glut of useless diversity, a heap of digital trash, the massive trivialization of all things?

Objects and backgrounds, authors and readers, designers and information users, all people, places and things, large and small, have become in effect, an immense computer: a system of existence. It is the story of the universal library come true.

Will quality and profundity be able to transcend digital democratization or will the romantic notion of one thing being better than another once and for all dematerialize along with the remaining languages on Earth?

The answers to these and other probing questions are naturally coming to a universal library near you, only a great many of the books are on backorder. They are expected sometime within the next hundred million years or so. It will be a world of informational bits unimaginable now. And we made it. God is here. You can find him in the card catalog, under "Details, The History of". And we already know that our names are on the title pages of all the books ever written. Our deeds past, present and future are recorded here. We are the designers. We are responsible.

This essay with all of its paradoxical quirks, in every language real and imaginary, with all of its ascribed authors, only takes up several billion volumes in the universal library. After all, it's only a small detail.....

*[Speech at the IDSA National Design Educators Conference, Atlanta,1995; Harvard University Graduate School of Design, 1997; and Aarhus School of Architecture, Denmark, 1998]*

# THE FLY ON THE CEILING

Every story starts with one or two ideas and goes somewhere, sometimes far away, sometimes not.

The words on this paper are a mental exercise in the far corner of a large box that contains design education, along with other thoughts on computers, professional practice and process. All reside in a larger box that holds industrial design. The boxes lie in a greater carton that contains the world...or tries to.

An empty container, like a box, a blank computer screen or a sheet of white paper, is a metaphor for the unknown. For people who create things, or draw pictures or write words, it's the frontier that marks the start of a project. I like to be friendly with the unknown, comfortable about not knowing what is going to happen. Given emptiness and a mind disposed to patience, more contents than you even want will soon materialize, but often in camouflage.

A book falls from a shelf. The phone rings. A letter arrives. As in a dream, images are slippery and vanish easily, or seem so ordinary that they just go completely unnoticed; but, it is certain that there will be a moment when suddenly, something unexpected occurs.

When I can't sleep on a hot night, I lie awake thinking about nothing in particular. On a certain night, a fly came through the window...

Its presence was announced by a break in the silence; its traversal of the room, by a minor Doppler shift in the buzzing sound. The fly swarmed around and then left. Several nights later a fly came back. I chose to think it was the same one. The fly inverted itself and stuck on the ceiling and remained there for 24 hours. I thought it was dead, but the next night it unstuck and danced around the ceiling for a time; in the morning it was gone.

A fly is comfortable upside down. It knows the three-dimensional world in a rich way: free to move on axes we're not used to. We can get closer to this knowlege in a small airplane. Balanced by gravity, lift, centifugal and centripetal force, sensitive to torque and velocity, we can turn and dive in the air in a more complex way than when we are glued to the ground. In the water the experience is similar, but in hydrodynamic slow-motion.

Having arrived at the ceiling, the fly is now upside down. Imagine, however, the puzzle of getting there. Was it an end-over-end flip, forward or back, or a sideways rotation on axis, in the docking maneuver from level flight to an inverted stop? How easily a fly crosses physical boundaries that we can't! From the tree through the window, down the stairs and out the door, a fly is a miniature explorer of N-dimensional space, a room with infinite number of doors to an infinity of other rooms. A mathematical equation and another mental exercise.

Theoretically, in the imagination, the tiny fly has possibilities of existence that seem infinite. It has many channels open, many possible paths to follow and the freedom to choose a path.

A fly: a small speck that appears and disappears. But at night, when a fly enters the room where a man is sleeping, it alters the environment of the man. When the fly is gone from the room, he may end up in the dreams of the sleeper. In the dream the fly becomes a ringing telephone or an old friend. The life of the sleeper changes. Just a little.

The fly reminded me of a particularly stubborn teacher of mine, observing me with its thousand-faceted eyes of little hexagons.

Staring down, it doesn't move for a long while: strangely patient, but capricious, ready to turn, buzz and lift off at any time. It still doesn't move...

A silent presence can be really annoying. And a fly has another annoying characteristic of not being very clean. But think of it as a flying metaphor disguised as a thought. Like a fly, a thought is very often not clean, often unformed and illogical. It buzzes through our heads like an insect. A fly can land on our ankle or on top of our head and refuse to go away. A good teacher, like a fly, has these sticky characteristics, landing inverted on the ceiling of the student's room, so to speak. Or on his shoulder. A reminder. The tiny explorer is a reminder to a student who wants to fly and see the world from above. The fly is small, but very powerful. This little traveller seems to have a definite penchant for discovery.

In a mindspace, all the infinite doorways represent ways of looking at things, as long as the doors are open, or at least have handles on them. When you pass through, the ceiling may become the floor, or there may be nothing at all. At first inspection, that is. A fly is a speck on the ceiling until you magnify it and observe the extent of its mechanism. A fly enters a territory with the knowlege that he may soon be upside down, and delights in it. We don't generally do that, expecting dimensional stability when our feet are on the ground.

If we say that a fly is a black speck on the ceiling, we also have to agree that all black specks are not flies! So we have to look carefully at each one, if we are truly curious. Like sound. At low volume levels on an old record player, heard through a thick plaster wall, the flute, the violin, and a human voice all sound very much the same. On a sensitive oscilloscope, however, we see an architecture of overtones which gives a special identity to every sound.

So you look up at a fly on the ceiling and you see only a speck. Even from close up, though, you can't see the lattice of its compound eyes.

Look down from 2500 feet above land and a human being will also look like a speck. You can't see the color of someone's skin, find out if they are men or women, or listen to their thoughts. Of course, all insects become totally invisible from here.

From space, all humans are totally invisible. The eye can resolve large countries, but the lines that divide them are erased. There is no homelessness, poverty or unrest. We cannot see political prisoners, a damaged environment or national holidays. There is no architecture or literature. No madness or creativity. No design.

Even under a magnifying glass, where you can see the complex structure of a fly's wing, you cannot see DNA or an atom of helium. Should we ignore what we cannot see with the unaided eye? We can try.

We often do. Until we suddenly come face-to-face with a killer disease or discover the tides.

In true N-dimensional space, no parameter can be ignored, even when its value is zero. That is to say, a locked door is still, in fact, a door. Like mixing paint, each drop of pure color contributes a component which can be detected in the final pigment. Education is like that, too.

When a student asks a question, what dimensions of the answer do you give? What dimensions do you know? We talk so easily about cost, materials, theory, form, function and styling, but what about aesthetics, connotation, resourcefulness and social conscience. It is when a design is infused with alot of interrelated dimensions that it is most successful – we smile, knowing intuitively, then, that it is good. A design of many dimensions is satisfying, full of subtlety. These subtleties are part of the richness of life. Without them, what's the point of design?

Whether design is a way of life or simply a job, I do not know. Sometimes, in a certain philosophical mood, like an imaginary fly with anti-gravity shoes on an inverted plane, I think there is no such thing as design at all. Whether I'm in my studio or someplace far away, during the day or late at night, there are elements of design everywhere in my life, and naturally, elements of my life everywhere in the work I do.

In a similar way, it really should surprise no one that design is not very different from other professions. Whereas the medium may be visual, the basic activity of studying and applying knowlege makes designers resemble mechanics and doctors, computer programmers or writers. What's the difference between brilliant logic and a beautiful car, a stunning performance and microsurgery? It is as tantalizing to a designer, as to anyone, to think that he can change the world. The exhuberance of creating something, added to the multiplying machine of mass production, makes a sense of power that is irresistible. It is natural that it should be so. Mass production has made it possible for a designer to leave behind artifacts; at best this means that an inspired act of creation can be shared with many people and endure for a time. It is also a noble human desire to express oneself and to pass on knowlege, or mementos of knowlege.

Objects, because they are solid and tangible, live on easily – that is, until they get broken, used up, or thrown away. This makes them somewhat tough as compared to more vulnerable acts of creation like words or music, which can be easily forgotten, whose levels of abstraction and finesse can be so varied, and whose performance, as in a play or concert lasting for a short time, are so fragile and beautiful, evanescent and changeable, subject to interpretation – qualities making demands on the audience, but often with profound reward. That great intangible acts of creation can also endure is a testimony to the dimension of the mind.

So, after all, it is precisely those things about design that seem most prosaic that turn out to be the most wonderful. The similarities of design to other fields should be celebrated, rather than picking at the differences. All acts of creation are in fact the same. Le Corbusier called cathedrals "acts of optimism". So too are the works of Citröen, Rutan, and Eames, in the company, of course, of Shakespeare and Brahms, Isaac Newton and Jonas Salk. And these are no different from the smallest or largest human effort to acheive, like microchips and cognac, reading a book or baking a cake. Acts of optimism draw on so many human parameters, and yet they are so simple... the childlike impulse to do something and be proud of it. There is no difference between creativity and survival: a fly on the ceiling is no less a miracle than Niagara Falls.

With this in mind, consider that educating a designer is no different from the eduction of anybody else, technical details notwithstanding. To say that a designer should be broadly educated is a convenient truism. But everyone should be broadly educated. A larger dose of the humanities for a designer would be good; so would eating more broccoli. But the metabolism of civilization finds its own course, and it's hard to divert it with a small change in diet.

The brain is capable of many kinds of informational metabolism. You don't have to put design directly into the brain to get design out. Feed the brain and let the brain feed the design. Feed our souls and our souls feed life. A soulless civilization is no civilization at all. That's the job of education that somehow we have to keep in mind and try to give to students. What we do about it is a matter of choice. But being aware of this is not a matter of choice at all.

Teachers and students need better rapport. Students have absolutely to be treated with respect, for their individual interests, character and learning process. A student is not an empty box, even though the contents are sometimes hidden. While it is trite to say so, sometimes the best talks I have had with students have not been about design at all.

Preparing for the future is another subplot of education; but the future does not disconnect from the past so easily. It's more realistic, if poetic, to say that the present extends forwards and backwards, like a colored liquid flowing from a pitcher onto a wooden table. The whole surface, like time, is soon tinted in many shades. Some things will never change. Humanity and metabolism, if they can be kept from drowning or choking in pollution remain noble and constant. Part of the nobility resides in education. It is the pipeline for important intangibles like curiosity, open-mindedness, patience, wit, spontaneity, richness and imagination: hard to teach, if not impossible. But they are to be sought after and celebrated when found. Passing on technical information is easy. Teaching a student to dream is not. Watching television is easy. Concentrating on a fly on the ceiling is not.

Teachers and students are educational comrades. Students have to maintain the motivation to do things, while teachers preserve the mature wish to share accumulated knowlege. The combination of these, and respect for both, makes education...in any field. A teacher has only the advantage of time and observation of the experiments of being alive; nevertheless, both students and teachers can be children, colleagues, risk takers, explorers and geniuses. If wisdom comes from the results of experiments, this means we have to be good experimenters. And good experimenters are good observers, and fluent enough in N-dimensional space to interpret the results of experiments in the broadest possible way. So it is that a fly on the ceiling is an opportunity. With the empty container of curiosity to trap the fly, we get a chance to observe him for a time. We need a good net and a good eye. A glass slide and a microscope. A clear dark night and our imagination.

Curiosity comes from childhood. We ought to be encouraging students to keep their curiosity and give some validity to the fact that that is what motivates us. And the motivation to make things is universal, crossing the lines the professions have drawn. It surprised me very much that people in Europe rarely ask you what you do at first meeting. Here, when you meet a person, you almost always say, "What do you do?" ...as if what we do really defines who we are. And just that simple attitude leads us back to a discovery about education. To repeat, we may not know enough about our students. And they don't know enough about us. In line with that it's possible that we don't know enough about ourselves. Knowlege, like an answer to a question, is a broken line, the path of a winged thought, an unpackaged quantum, a relative of the order Diptera, which buzzes all over the place, looking for a place to land.

I prefer to leave the debate about the process of design to others. Further analysis may not change the way we do things anyway. The basics remain immutable. Ideally, somehow, the best ideas are still the ones that just seem to pop out of nowhere. We should know how to develop an idea – that's of course very useful – but before that we should be able to recognize ideas and know where to find them. Sometimes the best way is just to close your eyes. Like in a dream. In the imagination, there is a big room. With lots of doors and windows. In the room are many powerful tools, ready to use. All we have to do is know that they're there. So the next time, on a beautiful summer evening, when a fly comes into the room through the window and lands on the ceiling, you just look up, laughing, and say, "What took you so long?!"

*[Speech at the IDSA National Design Educators Conference, Pasadena, 1990 - published in Design Management Journal, 1992]*

# IN THE END THERE WAS THE WORD

*An Essay on the Strange*
*Co-existence of Verbal and Visual Ideas in Design*

OkjwonfglslksAalskjhfuieuhpiuhlwvbyviverhb unifggvexyhnikp,mjvrxffgdfjubvggfdkkvbbhlm xcxcxccsgfeyuonpomwq2wuerpuhlkjlkjslkjhflkj sdflkjsdflasdlhasdfkasdfppoijhfpsijf;kjkjhflsjhlk jhdflkjsjfjhdjjwihfuisjhdbmncvbmnt riyudsjvjh dkhgdkjhdjjjhgkjjhfkjjhf..............Here I am, facing a huge bowl of alphabet soup of imposing diameter. Can you see it? It is my crystal ball of the future of design only it is in the form of a linguistic soup. I find, here among the letters I have been observing, that the language of literature is merging with the language of design. Paradox, mystery, semantics, contradiction, meaning, symbology, narrative!!! Have you heard these same words used to talk about design? I ask myself what's behind the hunger for meaning in objects of manufacture? And I'm wondering if this is just the edge of metaphysical black hole, a door to an exclusive club for the inner circle of design? Now, in the metamorphosing mind of the designer/ intellectual, the critic/professor, the aesthete/ executive,  the parallel realities of the hardware store and the library, the color wheel and conjugations of verbs,   the architecture of a computer chip and books have become linked, it would appear. In this dialogue between the 'talking object' and the designer/ raconteur, what is being said and who is listening? Where does this leave the consumer, the client, the human of human factors, the man on the street of urban society? What's the relevance of all this and what happened to the good old days when design's alleged purpose was the solving of technical problems and making things look good?? Yes, it's going to be an essay asking questions.

Welcome to the nineties. As a teacher of design, in trying to find insight into the process of creativity, I often find myself likening design to story-telling. This is not a new idea, but the metaphor seems to fit and it is broad enough to admit to the design of objects the richness of human experience which words can bring to literature. Yet as much as I am inclined to poetry and out-of-the-way explanations of how I see things, I am also the first to admit that sometimes "a cigar is just a cigar". A quick reading of Tom Wolfe's scathing satire on art criticism, "The Painted Word" and you will certainly be more careful, as a designer/artist/critic/teacher, what exactly it is you say! (no matter what you might actually think!!). To quote Wolfe:

> *A curious change was taking place at the very core of being a painter. Early Modernism had been a reaction to 19th century realism, but Abstract Expressionism... was an abstraction of an abstraction, a diagram of a diagram--and a diagram of a diagram is metaphysics...Metaphysics can be dazzling--as dazzling as the Scholastics and their wing commands of Angels. But somehow the ethereal little dears are inapprehensible without words. In short, the new order of things in the art world was: first you get the Word, and then you can see.*

Listen to criticism these days and you see where all this is leading: to a strange state of obfuscation where people seem not to be able to say what they mean, see what they are saying or indeed have nothing to say at all. Here's a selection from judges' comments in a recent Design Review Competition:

> *These (bicyclist's water bottles) offer a remarkably refreshing break from the standard sports language of neon colors and racing stripes. They are well thought-out objects in their own right. I wouldn't mind having them around even if I didn't own a bicycle. Their attention to detail has transformed these simple products into outstanding objects...and as we all know, it's a lot harder to get simple things right.*

Industrial design is of course not the only field where language now has an eerie presence. For a quick revealing trip into a cloud of words, read the work of a current architectural historian or attend a student presentation at an architecture school! One student at Harvard said:

> *Whenever people lose power--and certainly the phenomenon of architects losing power or not understanding power extends way beyond the schools--they start to create a magical language that no one else can understand, as if by hoarding the magic you could also somehow hoard the power.*

Outside the arts, the phenomenon of word pollution is well know. Talk to a lawyer or watch your elected leaders on television!! But wait a minute!! In design, the real issue is not the rampant misuse of language or declining literacy in the population so much as the question of whether the simple pleasures and experiences (verbal and non-verbal) in life are no longer accessible to us, and whether what we see, feel, and think now has to be made artificially complicated by layering, combination, narration, or whatever, in order for us to see these experiences as profound and satisfying. Think about it while we take a rather large detour...................

Lately, when I ask myself a big question, I write about it. I sit at this keyboard, staring into bluish-white cyberspace, contemplating whether I am advancing any state-of-the-art or just contributing to a mammoth pile of refuse composed of words and theories. "What is going on in design?" was a question which came up recently with respect to a major design event in San Francisco, held last August: the international, once-every-four-year version of the annual conference of the Industrial Designers Society of America.

At any conference, it is my personal style to sit at the back of the room (ready for hasty escape if required) and if possible to use this time to think. In San Francisco, during the flow of expected "design-words" in the introductory speeches I played a little game. I mentally substituted the word "plumbing" for "design" whenever it was said. (Surprisingly, it didn't make much difference in meaning.) In all this amusement I began to wonder if this conference would have some original contributions? There was no doubt of this in the featured speech of James Burke (Author/filmmaker of the BBC "Connections" TV series linking historical events, design and invention). Here was an unbelievable hour of symphonic monologue, a performance piece of concept and prose, apotheosis of the Word in its finest sense, delivered as a lecture (significantly!) without slides, video, computer, overhead transparency, photocopied handout or other multi-media prop. Daring, interesting and telling. When it was over, like a rendition of a Mahler song or a *grande bouffe*, where afterwards you only remember that you had heard or eaten well. The reality of it became a warm memory in time. Consider: A totally verbal presentation, a speech/performance, about visual design, provoking non-verbal, experiential reaction and a feeling of satiety and understanding, not just a memory of a string of words.

(Perhaps the beauty of simple expression is not dead; and perhaps "word" <u>has</u> a rightful place in "design" after all. I wonder.)

Disappointment would then follow. Hartmut Esslinger (frogdesign) spouted terminology starting with the letters D..E..S..I..G..N. (Spelling is, by the way, a fairly <u>primitive</u> component in the toolbox of the designer literati. This tool is from kindergarten!!) These "d.e.s.i.g.n.w.o.r.d.s." were offered as "concepts", however, in current design thinking. It is funny how "concept" aspires to some higher plane than the simple word "idea"; "concepts" form in the air, somehow, when there is enough vapor floating about to let a heavy verbal cloud condense to acid rain. (Why don't I like concepts?) One Japanese speaker called himself a "conceptor": product designer Naoki Sakai, for whom form only follows cultural/ marketing jargon. His interpretation of the "cultural collective unconscious" seemed to be nothing more than meaningless words trying to describe the arrhythmic heartbeat of consumerism and nostalgia. (Why don't I like Elvis?) Then, for a second notable moment in this conference: Frank Gehry, one of the most original, anti-intellectual, architects working today, presented his latest projects, the Disney Concert Hall for Los Angeles and a giant outdoor fish sculpture for Barcelona. Later in the symposium, the current state of design education was discussed. Unfortunately I was daydreaming by this time, so I only overheard mention of product semantics being just the beginning of a forecast of a greater dialogue with future products and their users. This dislodged me from my reverie. What planet am I on? I listened to my watch. It only ticked. It said nothing. I was, for a moment, somewhat relieved. (I don't want to talk to my watch, or have it talk to me!)

And now for the fun: this symposium's major social festivity was held at the <u>Exploratorium</u>, San Francisco's well-known "hands-on", "every exhibit works", "its OK to touch everything" children's science museum. I had several reactions. First, this wonderful museum was a great site for a party; its "faux-classical" architecture (built as part of the Pan-American Exposition of 1915, then never demolished) and rough-hewn exhibits clashed compellingly, and the contrast provided a hospitable environment

for the intellectual contortions of design critique and "concept" of the symposium itself (held in a typically boring hotel conference room) which floated serenely out of reach, like smoke along the high rafters, while the attendees pondered the miracles of science. Second, the exhibits and revelers both came alive that evening, blending into happy interaction, playing, responding, informing each other. (Why do conferences have to be so dreary?) One would only have hoped to encounter a greater number international designers (perhaps who would rather be at the beach in August) at a purportedly international symposium, and that the conference itself were held in a more provocative venue, one more challenging sensually, intellectually and architecturally. Surely San Francisco could have offered up one of these.

Now back to work...........

One of my favorite things is an unsolved puzzle. Obviously we live in a world rich in paradox, a grand universe (and daily life as well) of irony and layers of meaning. The revealing indicators for me are in how people are thinking and speaking about design. Listen to what a friend just wrote about architect, Eric Moss: "He is a messenger of doubt rather than certainty...His strategy...was to interrogate and punctuate...with unique spatial episodes." You recognize here, of course, the vocabulary of literature. Good-bye well-worn and familiar trope that "form follows function"; hello "form follows idea". Art and architecture have already welcomed this literary rhetoric, but it has been much less frequently represented in design criticism. The machinery of this cosmos of design has changed, along with its language. I can't escape it. Listen to what I just wrote: The upheaval distorts the Cartesian grid, with its limits and boundaries, clarity and constraint, its x and y, into fractal geometry, string theory and the physics of weather. A butterfly lands on a leaf in Kansas and it rains in L.A.! The shapes of objects have curved to fit a decidedly non-Euclidean mold and mind-set. Design has become literate, as the cultural vibrations in the air resonate with the paradoxes of life the '90s where, I conclude, that more than "design following idea", "form follows word." (Wow!)

"Form follows Word" has in a sense been around for a while. You've seen it in Futurism, Dada, and Constructivism. Typography and graphic design operate on this aphorism, which in three innocent words ties visual language and verbal language, seeing and reading. Of this, Katherine McCoy (Co-chairman of Design, Cranbrook Academy of Art) writes:

> The early Modernists discovered that text can be seen as well as read, as the Futurists experimental poetry proved. And images can be read. The Neolithic cave painters at Lascaux knew this, as have most painters throughout history. This process has been reconfirmed by the Surrealists, by graphic designers since the 1930's... Many early Modernists saw themselves as integrated creators of communications, balancing the identities of artist, designer, businessman and craftsman, exploring all four modes.

Sophisticated graphics take on multiple meanings on second and third readings, depending on who you are and how carefully you read, and based on the complexity of actual content or meaning derived from advertising, form, or politics. Fine details of typography are appreciated only by cognoscenti (other designers), but the subtleties of the verbal content might go unnoticed by the visual brain and yet have dramatic import to a literary eye.

Somehow I want to make sense of all this. My inclination is to appreciate all creative work multifariously and to explore any tangent, intellectual, literate or artistic  idea spun off by any such work. An opera has its score and libretto; each can be appreciated separately, of course, but the full impact of an opera derives from its combined excitement of <u>all</u> of the senses. In what other form of art are so many different kinds of content represented? Architecture, stage design, music, language, literature, theater and costume are the essential dimensions of opera. (and of human experience!!)  Many people listen to opera in foreign languages without understanding the words, for example, showing that this art form is so rich that it can be incompletely understood and yet deeply satisfying. Listening to a performance of opera on radio removes important dimensions, yet great music, beautiful voices and a good plot conjure up images.

Can product design take on the magnificence of opera, or  manifest the same communication as typography? Its an intriguing important question. I (and a number of contemporaries, as teachers and designers) have explored the notion of conceptual design, which is nothing more than "form follows idea". It is sometimes an interesting way to teach students (design a coffee pot based on Shakespeare's Hamlet), but it is a method often misunderstood.

Notably, conceptual design thinking is being promoted at the corporate level also, in an attempt to stimulate creativity in companies where the stultifying hierarchy and exigencies of day-to-day business lead to stasis. At an intellectual level, among a certain few, conceptual design has become exciting, if somewhat esoteric. Of course, most of the rest of the world thinks this approach is simply stupid. That's why I ask my questions. Is there enough depth of experience possible in ordinary objects of manufacture to justify intellectual and conceptual interpretations? Or, again, are humans so out of touch with human qualities, so lonely and hungry in this great universe, that we pile up layers of complexity everywhere, even on a coffeepot, to titillate ourselves or to make all things seem important, and therefore make life more profound?

However you answer the "big" questions, you can be sure that there are also a lot of interesting smaller issues in design. One is called THE INTERFACE. It seem to be an area of real concern as products become more complicated. It started with computers, but now extends to bankomats and can openers. How <u>should</u> humans interact with machines?

At present, obviously, it is thought that some kind of language is required. This communication used to be in the form of someone teaching you how to use a certain machine. If you were independently minded, you could read the owner's manual. Now there are learning curves, tutorials and simulations. Computers talk to themselves internally with one language, are programmed by humans with another, and then users employ a third at the interface of human, machine and task. It is at this interface that the promise of any meaningful connections between design and word and between human and machine becomes possible. As the Industrial Age evolves into the Information Age, it is clear that this evolution is one of language. Where there is language, there is human expression.

And as new expression demands new vocabulary, so does new creation insist on new tools. The calculator and ruler give way to the dictionary and CAD. Computers have conveniently merged the content of word and picture into indistinguishable bits. We talk of multimedia, as if a single medium isn't enough, and levels of meaning and multiple 'readings' of visual work must be complex in order somehow to be understandable! What a paradox! (It was once the opposite. Remember simplicity?) The linking of form and word not only makes a chain, but a vast array in hyperspace of possible meanings!! Architects and writers, graphic designers and critics, orators and magicians, scientists and artists, literati and consumers, professors and musicians are playing out the big bang in this crazy word-and-picture universe. A parody of Karl Marx: all that was solid has dematerialized

into word! What a planet this is!! We have been born in interesting times! Language is changing the world!!

I read a very odd assortment of periodicals each month, searching for ideas and answers. This month, in *Innovation*, the journal of the Industrial Designers Society of America, I found an interview with six design managers of various corporate design departments. One said:

> *Being a good listener is crucial. Designers must be able to understand where someone else is coming from while not giving up their own perspective...We've learned that lesson...because we've had to listen and understand a different language and culture. Engineering, marketing, finance and planning are just that, foreign cultures.*

This has been conventional wisdom in product design. "Learn the language of the other players in the game!" Consider the funny circumstance where designers would not have to justify their own existence defensively to the foreign culture of business. Designers wouldn't then wear the usual suits and neckties. Business people might learn to speak about form and function, criticize the proportions of the latest portable CD player, and perhaps wear black clothes to meetings where they would beg busy designers for the chance to invest a few bucks in their latest design. (This is not imaginable, is it?) The language of this situation is perhaps too foreign to conceive!

Now for the punch line: Language, say in the form of design criticism, can itself be an art form, an artifact of literature, like poetry. But, when "form follows word", criticism, as word by definition, precedes what is criticized, and here the vessel of process is upended. What spills out into product design is liquid paradox, and a desperate society doesn't handle paradox very well. People, the planet, and the future all need the attention of designers using their brains on some fairly ugly problems. More than that, I would like to imagine a time when the collective voice just utters a simple AH! responding to a product or design which proclaims its solid worth to humanity. It would be a reassuring twist on the idea of criticism to hear public outcry or unabashed gut-level approval. If only there were a forum for this. Perhaps the next time there is an international conference on design...............

Emilio Ambasz wrote in ID magazine last September:

*I believe that designers at this point in time can find more truth and inspiration in design derived from the body than from the hackneyed game of cultural semantics. Language is a very seductive but treacherous device...* I wonder. These thoughts have sent me back to my own personal library. I'm still looking for answers to my questions. I have been reading more about typography, where Word inhabits Art and art inhabits word, and also playing with games like palindromes and anagrams, where Design gives form to Words. From the library, confused as ever, I leave you with this conundrum:

Take the letters in D.E.S.I.G.N. A.S. W.O.R.D, rearrange them, and you get N.E.W. S.O.R.D.I.D. G.A.S!

*[Speech at University of Wisconsin-Stout, Department of Design, 1992 - published in the regional newsletter of the Industrial Designers Society, 1992 and in extended form in the design journal Dom & Wnetrze, Warsaw, 1993]*

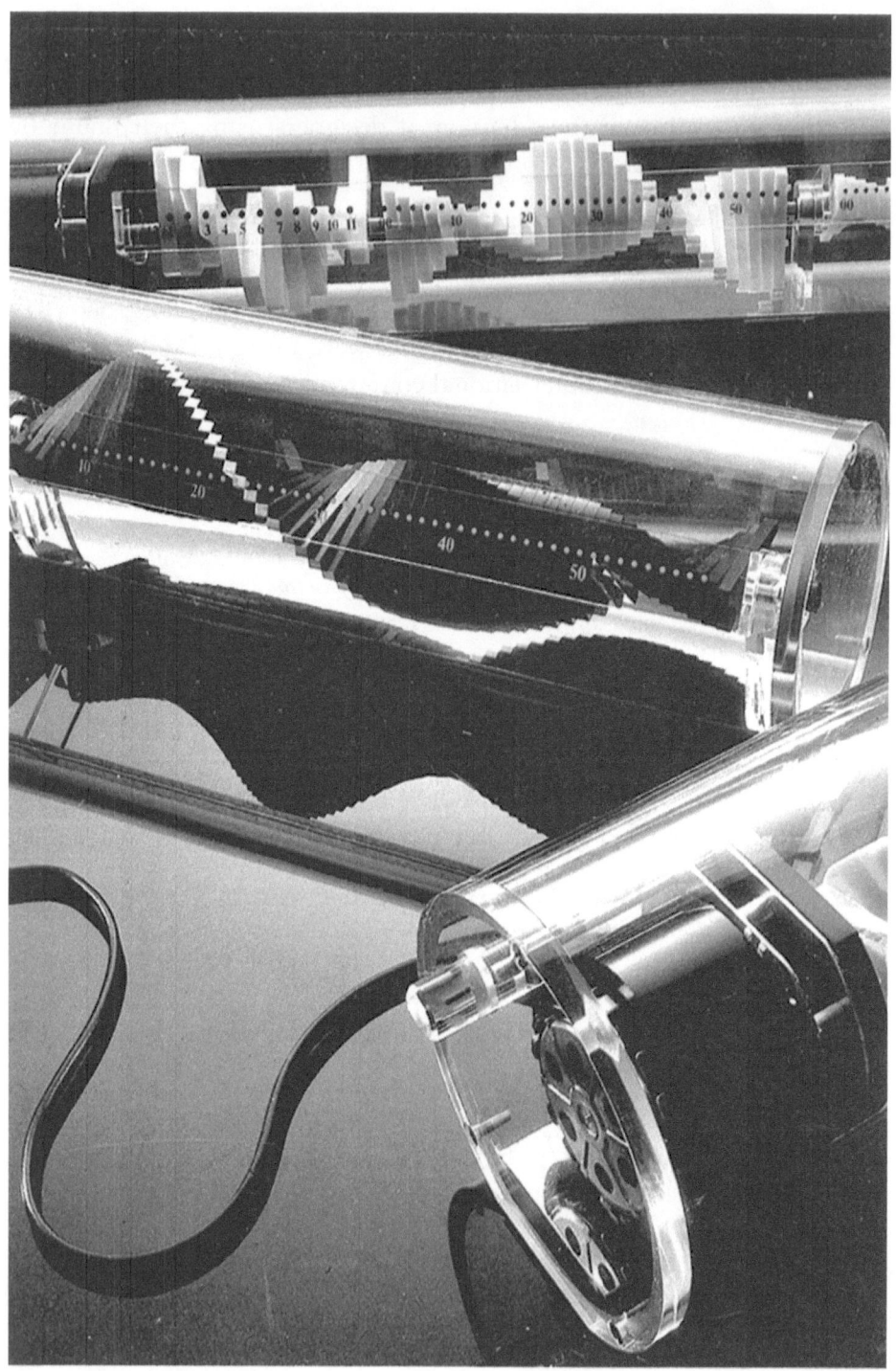

# SENTIMENTAL MASS PRODUCTION

I have at some point considered the notion that design is a narrative process, with designers as authors of the great stories linking objects and human beings. These are the stories of environment, character, poetry and time, sentimental wanderings of thought and form where inanimate and animate objects are interwoven in a lyrical biology and structure. This is how I got started in industrial design.

In the chain of being linking sub-atomic particles to mankind, there is something missing: the object – extension of man, elusive artifact of evolution! Objects come alive, children of the designer-mind as evidence of our existence, in many cases long after we are gone. Just as DNA has a language, the mass-produced object, by its dissemination throughout the world, also becomes a powerful device for communication. This dynamic quality of the secret life of objects vibrates within every object, large and small.

Far from that operating room where design lies on the table for surgery, where men in white try to solve the technical problems which they themselves conceive, I'm thinking that the vibrant heart of design lies elsewhere, in the making of objects. This thought originates in the mind of a designer as the deep need for a conversation with civilization, the desire to say something – and it often starts with a BIG IDEA.

My idea arrived in 1976, while I was in Japan working as an architect. We worked long hours, but sometimes there were great rewards. At a certain point, I suddenly had a hunger for a really small and personal project, so I decided to consider a different way of telling time! I found that after months in a strange land, one begins to absorb cultural information very rapidly, out of a need for understanding. In Tokyo, the atmosphere crackled with architecture and symbols, society, objects, as well as a different relationship with time. A culture where natural disasters formed the shape of the city (and where until 1873 time was measured by hours which varied in length from day to day, through the seasons of expanding and contracting daylight) cannot fail to give a designer certain ideas.

I had in mind a "color clock", a cylinder of many illuminated bands, with a helical mechanism inside to sequence the lights with an ordinary motor. This prototype in my mind stimulated the further thought that the mechanism itself might be an interesting sculptural "thing", and that most people wouldn't bother about "blue minutes after pink o'clock", or being "yellow minutes late for a meeting". In parentheses, I also realized that an object can force users into learning a different language and that this demand easily makes enemies of consumers.

So, a helical clock was born. Named Helix, it was really just a machine for spinning rotary motion into linear motion, a Nautilus chronometer, seashell of time, a wheel rolling down the ramp of the space-time continuum, a well-behaved spiral advancing forever, resetting itself with periodic certainty, a solidly mathematical spiral staircase to infinity.

As I have said: far from the world of "problem solving as we know it", I have found that the heart of design lies in the lyrical and sometimes capricious nature of objects. Design ideas form a rich soup, with ingredients bubbling to the surface at random from the invisible depths at the bottom of the pot where they can burn and be destroyed if the flame is too high, or take on the color of the surrounding broth, the ooze in which ideas can easily disappear. The process, nevertheless, is frequently nourishing – but once in a while one gets indigestion, or worse, food poisoning.

The soup in question here is a helical soup. In this pot are a year's worth of prototypes and the steep learning curve of a new field with its own language and materials; but I was still guided by the lyrical impulse, a kind of childlike wonder about objects and their making. This period included flirtation with expressive form, materializing as a celebration of seconds. Hours move very slowly in a clock, measuring time in a very unrewarding way. I wanted more – more drama, more action – so I made three helical rotors and made the one which shows seconds very long, in sixty discreet segments, and then accentuated it with a polished mirror base to reflect the sensuous rhythm of the passage of time.

I decided to show this prototype to another human being. My friend saw this funny machine, actually liked it, and said he would like to buy one. (This is called "market research", by the way).

My studio was in a garage, and I say "studio" because of the romance of this word. A studio can be anywhere, or anything – it is a special architecture of the mind. I showed Helix to a university professor of business. Six students in his class signed up to help me research the feasibility of bringing the Helix to market. "Market", like "studio", is another romantic, institution. It is, I can tell you, "the market" which animates products; in the market the designer can hear the sweet songs of fame, fortune and affection for one's work. I loved the smooth sound of the word "entrepreneur" and remember the pride of anticipated ownership of this title; but my real dream was a chimney, and the heavy cloud of particles of object-making, the industrial cigar, belching evidence into the atmosphere over my fantasy factory, proclaiming in the most lyrical words of all:  MASS PRODUCTION!

Now let me give you an observation: I believe that all objects are like penguins: frolicking on the assembly line, anticipating the mating ritual with other parts, totally comfortable where it's cold, at home on land or at sea; objects are just like penguins struggling for the shore, longing to swim and play. For objects, that Great Ocean is, of course, the Sea of Commerce.

So here were six students eager to put me in business. We photographed the prototypes, visited retail stores, interviewed owners, tried to price parts, learned of exotic processes and materials, and went to trade shows. I laugh now, but these were ardent efforts, by new entrepreneurs wearing fictional three-piece suits, smoking fictional cigars, with light bulbs and dreams in their heads, inventing grand plans.

We would become mass producers, another link in the great chain of being: makers of objects. But then I called a phone number in Boston.

I had learned of a little two-man company, an architect and a physicist who lived the dream of cigars and light bulbs, mass producers of clocks which employed polarized filters to make the face change color as time passed. (Sound familiar? Ideas, like twins, always come in pairs.)

I took the red eye. They wanted to see the Helix clock. The great moment of this visit was the factory. Machines everywhere, numerically controlled lathes and mills, grinders and drill presses, hand tools and testing racks, strange-looking fixtures and a definite mood that here was a place where man and machine were equals. This was an alchemical place where ideas transmuted into objects, like lead into gold, a place where sea lions would play, where products would jump from their boxes, dancing through the night to the tunes of an orchestra of cast aluminum instruments or a mighty pipe organ, let's say a pipe organ of acrylic tubes of every diameter and wall thickness. This was a place I wanted to be.

We talked of licensing, production costs, sales, materials, patents and royalties. We decided to call the lawyers: it was time to make a deal. It became a 22-page agreement. It went like this: "In consideration of one dollar, paid by the Licensee to the Licensor, the receipt of which is herein acknowledged, the parties agree as follows... Licensee shall place on each of the Licensed products the following acknowledgement: 'designed by Steve Diskin' in a location on such Licensed Product that is visible to the naked eye when such product is in ordinary use." Sea lions on rocks by the sea barked loudly. The objects were laughing, so were the lawyers.

Parts for five prototypes were made on a pantograph mill and carefully assembled into the finished clock. One hundred and two little hand-made parts. Revolution in the streets of objects! The solution would come from a farm in Connecticut. where a small injection molding company offered to make these little segments. Cows stuck their heads through the window and mooed. Parts began to fill a cardboard box. Registration pins and holes in each part made assembly much easier. Tight angular tolerances had to be maintained – sixty segments to make one 360-degree revolution, not 361. We were nervous. The cows were nervous. We had to decide what color to make these parts.

Black and yellow were proposed. Then I said: "chrome." Silence. Then enthusiasm! The physicist took us to MIT and put one of the rotors under a huge bell jar in a lab and vaporized a little piece of aluminum in an exquisite, airless void. The pump burbled, the aluminum was consumed. Scientists laughed.

Chrome, black and yellow production prototypes went to the LA gift show. Orders were taken. Helix would be shipped in time for Christmas! I spent weeks in Boston at the factory, designing fixtures for hot stamping the rotors, milling endcaps, breathing the heady vapors in the factory – the smell of incipient mass production. Labels were applied to the newborn clocks: "designed by Steve Diskin" would indeed be visible to the naked eye when the product was in normal use. The first unit went to Beverly Hills. I waited clandestinely in the store listening for comments. "I hate this thing," a mother told her 12- year old son, who openly coveted serial number 1. "It makes me so mad." A week later I heard from the owner of the store that number 1 was sold, and to a noted luminary at that – Stevie Wonder! Who says that there is no poetry in mass production!

Shipping started, but then disaster struck. Inadequate packaging failed to protect the object inside. Gravity, inertia and momentum intersected; matter and energy collided full force. A Helix in a box went to the testing laboratory. It sustained nine G's as it hit the floor. This at last forced into existence a container which swaddled the newborn in an additional cocoon of plastic bubbles.

"Shipping": it's the third panel in a medieval triptych of object-making, hinged to the iconic representations of "Sales" and "Production". Shipping is descended from the altar of the prototype, through the fury of mass production, the wild meiosis of sub-assemblies and parts, backstage at the drama of shipping, directed by the numerology of purchase orders, invoices and packing slips – the chronicles of product lives. Designer-makers look on wistfully as friendly birds leave the nest. Ultimately, shipping is a form of flight, in all the meanings of the word.

In the meantime, Helix appeared in stores, catalogs, magazines and newspapers. After a year, difficulties in production were gradually resolved. And at this moment the company was sold. The new owners weren't cigar smoking light-bulb heads at all, but decaffeinated and pasteurized, gold-chained businessmen. They saw balance sheets where smokestacks should have been. The music of the factory became silence. It would be a matter of time, so to speak, before the Licensor and the Licensee would part company. Fewer than 1000 clocks would be sold.

There would also be no going back. In 1980 I made another decision. I would be a designer-maker, a manufacturer. Helix had been my rite of passage into the mysteries of industrial design and now I can barely remember life before ID. It's like a pianist trying to remember the feeling of not being able to read music. In a 40 square-meter studio-factory, we subsequently produced thousands of new clocks, proudly displaying the label: "designed by Steve Diskin" and visible to the naked eye when the product was in normal use.

In small scale production, a designer-maker learns to distinguish the inevitable defects which make each object minutely different from the rest. Seeing so many of these little objects side-by-side while they were in the studio, I got to know the quirks of each one as if by name. And I ask myself: Is there any doubt that objects and designers commune at the workbench, the altar of creativity? Whenever I see a product with a scratch or a screw missing or a part which doesn't fit, rather than getting angry, I am reminded of mass production, and personality, environment, poetry, character and time. I love old products, discontinued products, defective products and, naturally, beautiful new products.

When I would make prototypes, and the studio would have already become a complete mess from the cutting, drilling, and sanding and painting of parts, I would always clear a sacred area on the workbench for a bit of soft cloth to make a ceremonial hearth for the rite of final assembly. With the sweet smell of paint (especially flat black) infusing the air in the studio, there would be the perfect parts, waiting. You hold a screwdriver reverentially when you assemble a prototype, and there is a glowing halo when the job is done. This is standard procedure at the altar of creativity.

But the real pulpit of object-making is in the factory. It was a moment of true serenity in the quality control room at a certain metal stamping plant as I, a designer admitted to the inner circle, and fabricator, micrometer in hand, admired the first article: production piece number one. The fabricator knew and admired the careful work of the designer and the designer respected the capability and experience of the fabricator, and both knew that the other knew. Both stood here on the same sacred spot. This altar demands recognition, and people who understand the life of objects know this. People who understand objects know that a car always runs better after it's washed. These people also understand computers and know that the battle at the man-machine interface involves not so much the humanization of machinery with friendlier software, but more the convincing of human beings that it's OK to coexist with objects.

What does all this mean? A corollary of the widely heard idea that small is beautiful is that small efforts are also beautiful. The executives of General Motors or Hitachi, like the owner of a one-man shop, have had ethereal dreams of the smokestacks of production, they feel the the primitive urges of the making of objects, they agonize over the minute technical details of finance and design, and watch with complex emotion as shipping disseminates the dream to the consuming populace. This is the life of the designer-maker.

The persistence of objects, and of the humans who design them, is given. I, in my own small corner of design, also know that I am not alone in what I think and do. Sea lions play, and trees will grow happily where the conditions of humidity are hospitable. Human beings dream, and billions and billions of the products we have inserted into a very interesting ecosystem of objects will dance the night away under beautiful halogen suns, in factories real and imagined, throughout the entire universe.

*[Speech at the Regional Conference of the Industrial Designers Society, Pacific Design Center, Los Angeles; Harvard University Graduate School of Design, 1997; Academy of Fine Arts, Warsaw, 1992; and during the Month of Design in Ljubljana, at the design firm Asobi, 2004 - published in the design journal Dom & Wnetrze, Warsaw, 1992, and Innovation, the journal of the Industrial Designers Society of America]*

# FEAR

I'm scared. I'm always a little bit scared. To have something to say and to say it well is not easy – and as usual, I wait until the last minute to prepare. Sometimes I believe it is so that I will have a maximum amount of time to think. And sometimes I think it is because I am scared. I'm scared that I have too many questions and not enough answers. I'm afraid I might be a poet and not an industrial designer! Or maybe not an architect.

I admit it. But one thing I have learned is that if you're not scared, you're not alive. If you're not scared, you're not really working. Creativity is supposed to feel quite awkward.

So in the last week or two, I started organizing a lecture and going through some slides of student work and some pictures of my own work as well. Then I decided to look at some things I had once written about design.

*I've been reading about Antarctica, and the last expedition of the British explorer Robert Scott. Back in the early 1900's, before radar, telecommunication, and NASA spacesuits, a trip to the Pole must have seemed as difficult as going to Mars. At a time when most of the Earth's surface had been charted, the interior of the continent of Antarctica was only a white circle at the 80th parallel, with a black dot at the south pole. Featureless and inhospitable, but at the same time beautiful and mysterious, this place must have represented an object of great fascination just like the future in general does for us. Scott's arrival at the edge of Antarctica was amid icebergs and fog crystals. Scott ascended in a balloon, up to 800 feet,*

*but saw endless snow to the horizon. At night he wrote: "Overhead a myriad*
*of stars irradiates the heavens while the aurora shimmers in tongues of flame*
*over the very zenith, then melting away in the moonlight."*

The poetry of this weird land was mixed with the extensive technical
planning of the venture: calculation of weight, location of camps along
the way, the animals and sleds, and timing. As you probably know, Scott
never returned. Not only that, he was remembered as the second man
to reach the South Pole.

• • • • •

This story made me think. For us as people who create things,
Antarctica is always there. When a new assignment starts, we go to
our office in our heads with our palette of skills and experience. And
there is the white circle – a napkin in a restaurant, a sheet of notebook
paper or a blank computer screen. Its a very exciting, sometimes tense
moment, when the pen hits the paper. Sometimes it feels like a matter
of life and death. It is a definition of excitement: a mixture of fear and
creativity.

Have you not felt PANIC sometimes at the beginning of a project?
Or in the dark hours of early morning had a disturbing project dream?
I have to assume it is the same story for all of us, more or less.

It's no wonder we feel this way. We are expected to be intellectual,
scientist, philosopher and artist, inventor and businessman, technological
guru and psychoanalyst. And we are expected to be really "cool" at the
same time. As architects, we have shaped the built environment; we
may be called upon to design a city plan or a small table. There are
people who have designed electrical power stations and refrigerators,
fabrics and lamps, common everyday products sports equipment and
packaging. It is no wonder we are a little bit crazy! But it is no excuse for
being so damned insecure about ourselves and for struggling so hard to
justify our existence as designers in the world. True, many people don't
understand the work we do. Many others understand but don't value it
and often don't want to pay for it. But take away our work and you will
find citizens with nothing to wear, no chair to sit on,  no place to live

and to a certain extent, nothing to do.

Together with our artist friends, our cousins who are musicians and writers and our colleagues in science who have made technological discoveries, even those who manage creative companies – together we can be creating the future of civilization!

A terrifying thought But if we don't do it, who will? Our unique and sometimes patchwork background, our diverse interests, our training, and our designerly way of thinking has to be put to use. Have designers arrived too late at the South Pole? We should be leading the expedition. Let's risk that we can do it!

I found an interesting article called "How Fear Kills Great Design" and there was a quote from a design manager at Apple Computer:

> *It's not enough for a product to deliver unique features at low cost. The design must tell a story that management can understand. Even at companies that encourage innovation, the fear factor makes it difficult to ship anything that departs from the status quo without that product story.*

What is this all about? I ask myself what's behind the hunger for meaning in objects of manufacture? Yet I also understand that narrative, or story, is they way that humans have communicated since the beginning. It is no wonder that designers who make things have a strong desire to say something. Perhaps it is often without words. So I have some questions: Has meaning gone out of our lives? Do we need more stuff to feel good? Don't we have anybody to talk to?

We get scared. So what do we do? We write reports, make theories. study what others have done, and in the extreme sacrifice ourselves to the whims of big business, solicit the ill-considered opinions of people in focus groups in super markets trying to give them what they think they want. And we contribute to a world of diminished expectations, of mediocrity, as we hide behind the façade of the word "professional". This cannot be the only answer.

We do have something to say. Let's raise the expectations about what is possible on planet Earth. We can do this. As designers, we are really teachers. We tell people a lot by what we design, about quality, creativity, innovation, function, ergonomics and humanity. The way to teach is by setting an example. Great teachers, to the extent they can, do not wait for permission. They experiment and explore with every tool at their disposal. They have a vision and a motivation which awakens them every morning, and sometimes late at night, with the desire to work.

That desire is a phone call from the creative process to you.

I am not sure what creativity really is, but one simple way to look at it is the unexpected juxtaposition of two things which didn't used to go together. Like two people who have just met. Cross two electrical wires and sometimes you get a spark. Or you could get killed!

We once were creative all the time, everyday, until someone said no.

I saw an exhibition of photographs of Albert Einstein. There were nine beautiful portraits and in eight of them Albert Einstein, arguably one of the greatest geniuses who ever lived, was wearing a formal suit. But in the ninth photograph he was wearing a black leather jacket and his hair was flying all over the place. What is more, he had a large smile on his face. It was the face of a child, which communicated special excitement, a sort of combination of fear and creativity. Al was about to ride a motorcycle.

The caption of this picture said that this was the only photograph in the series which was not posed by Einstein's wife!!!

*[Closing speech at the NorskForm Design Conference, Norwegian Industrial Designers Society, Oslo, 1996]*

# ANTARCTICA

Recently, I have been spending more time than usual thinking about the future, especially in our studio, where for about the last 3 years we have been designing, speculating, fantasizing, laughing about, eating, drinking and dreaming about the "office of the year 2000". But it wasn't until last week, driving down the Ventura Freeway that the reality of the office of the future really hit me. Its pretty crazy when you think about it. I was dictating this speech into a tiny black box, while zooming along at high speed in a vehicular cocoon that has a very low coefficient of drag, breathing cool conditioned air. Then the phone rang! Our office manager patched me in to a call from a colleague in Sacramento. When I got back to the studio, I faxed some sketches to Dayton, Ohio and relaxed to do some drawings on my Macintosh, which I keep in a funny prototype work station that looks like a wheelbarrow turned up on end. Its been a long time since I have drawn anything with a pencil, and the thought of working at a regular desk seems strange to me now. It's the future all right, call it the year 2000, and it's now. In ten years, when the numbers change from 19 to 20 we will only be that much more used to the new things we are already doing today.

Hopefully by then, we will understand a little bit more about the office environment, because even though we might get used to it over a period of time, the transition into the future of the workplace is not necessarily an easy one. I've read that we are doing more and more in teams. I understand that we are becoming "knowledge workers" with easy access to so much information; but sometimes I confess that I seem to "know" very little. As we get to 2000 we will be swamped with even more data and risk being somewhat overwhelmed by technology. In the face of this, teamwork may help us stay sane and human. Anyway, as an architect, industrial designer and, recently, professor, I would just like to say a few things about how to prepare for what's ahead. These rambling thoughts start with a quick visit to the South Pole!!

Often, after a long day with computers and the abstract world of design, I get a definite craving for the solid reality of a good book. Lately I've been reading about Antarctica, and the last expedition of the British explorer Robert Scott. Back in the early 1900's, before radar, telecommunication and NASA spacesuits, a trip to the Pole must have seemed as difficult as going to Mars. At a time when most of the Earth's surface had been charted, the interior of the continent of Antarctica was only a white circle at the 80th parallel with a black dot at the South Pole. Featureless and inhospitable, but at the same time beautiful and mysterious, this place must have represented an object of great fascination, just like the future in general does for us. Scott was an experienced sailor who had explored Antartica on a scientific expedition for the Royal Geographical Society. His final trek to the Pole, which turned out to be a devastating race against the Norweigan, Amundsen, is a gripping story.

Scott's first arrival at the edge of Antartica was amid icebergs and fog crystals. Scott ascended in a balloon, up to 800 feet, but saw endless snow to the horizon. At night he wrote: "Overhead a myraid of stars irradiates the heavens while the aurora shimmers in tongues of flame over the very zenith, then melting away in the moonlight."

The poetry of this weird land was mixed with the extensive technical planning of the venture: calculation of weight, location of camps along the way, the animals and sleds, and timing. Scott knew that it was not a one-man show, but an endeavor that required teamwork. Their spirits were high but the knowlege that Amundsen had also sailed for Antartica displaced their confidence with greed and self-centered competition. The race was on. Scott made some tactical errors. He had started the trip too late in the summer season. He brought ponies instead of dogs. Their strength-to-weight ratio was bad. Hooves faltered in the snow and ice, where as paws had no trouble. On January 17, 1911 Scott finally arrived at the Pole with hopefulness, only to find the black flag of Amundsen, who had arrived only one month earlier and was now on the way home. The rest of the account I leave for your own discovery. I'll just tell you that Scott never returned. He was a dead hero: The second man at the South Pole.

This story made me think about the lessons in it. In a remote way it's about educating ourselves for the future. What do we learn from all of this? For us as people who create things, Antartica will always be there. When a new assignment starts, we go to our office in our heads with our palette of skills and experience. And there is the white circle – a napkin in a restaurant, a sheet of notebook paper or a blank computer screen. It's a very exciting, sometimes tense moment, when the pen hits the paper. Sometimes it feels like our life is on the line. Literally.

Preparing for a venture of the magnitude of exploring Antartica may be a metaphor for planning for the future as designers. And lets assume that we are preparing to be designers for the office environment of the year 2000. A challenging expedition like this requires good equipment. Let's keep the equipment in a metaphorical toolbox for use in the office which we carry around with us in our heads.

These are the things I advise you to take with you into the future. In my own case, I carry both an architect's and product designer's toolbox. Its been very valuable to me to do so, and it leads me to the first tool you should have: scope. I like this word because it implies depth and breadth and talks about looking at things carefully and at different scales of magnification. At the edge of Antartica, just able to see the tiniest part of the great continent, Scott went up in a balloon struggling to broaden his view. Designers are explorers and should always be curious to see more and learn more. Hopefully, at a certain point, you can begin to combine what you know in different fields and focus this knowledge on a single problem. The Scott expedition drew upon a very wide scope of scientific observation, technical know-how, teamwork, management, emotion, and even poetry for its heroic effort.

A relative of scope is versatility. In addition to the basic thinking and drawing skills we learn as designers, we ought to have a repetoire of other skills as well. Knowlege of the properties of materials is one skill;

but books, music, movies, language, history, psychology are other areas of interest which can be very valuable in informing the design process. Alot of the understanding of the office of the future will come from how people behave and what people need, not simply from designing better furniture or more advanced machines. The best designer knows alot about life as well as about design.

The third useful tool, then, is experience. You have to try different things and go to different places. Travel is an excellent form of experience. Certainly, Scott would not have had the leadership ability and courage to survive Antartica had he not been an expert navigator and visitor to many strange lands on the way. This prepared him to be more at home with uncertainty and better able to understand new challenges and environments. Experience also involves meeting people and finding out what they are about. Working in a design office if one way. Talking to someone in a cafe in Italy is another.

Fourth in the toolbox comes risk. It is necessary to take risks. For us as designers this usually means risking failure. Scott's case is extreme of course. His tragic demise should not obscure his heroism, nor his enormous contribution to the scientific understanding of Antartica. This may translate into something useful for us – that great success can even come from a magnificent failure. Fortunately, school can provide a unique forum for taking risks with a safety net attached. A drawing for example. A seemingly perfect drawing may only be one that is traced over a lines that have been there before. You may be tracing the path of a deep rut. The first line leading to new and creative territory may be messy and broken. Draw it anyway. Let's not let our work, particularly our early work be so precious that we have nothing to learn from it.

Taking creative risks in school ultimately brings us to the judgement that comes from it, which in school often translates into grades. What grade we would give Robert Scott for example? His colleagues back in England gave him mostly A's, yet there were some who felt he should be penalized for not having made it back home to pick up his report card! Don't work just for grades, and don't work just to please your teachers.

Therefore, the final tool is assertiveness. Your work is for you and your education is for you. When teachers challenge you, challenge back. Its sort of like a game of pingpong. Neither student nor teacher gets anything when the other side of the table is vacant. Get to the point where you're really learning something. If what you hear sounds like wisdom, test it! If it holds up, use it!

Well, that's it. A designer's toolbox for the future. Maybe there is one more thing in it: let's leave a note not to take ourselves so seriously all the time. Ego has made governments corrupt, the environment ill, and millions of people miserable. If part of the future of the office lies in more teamwork and expanded knowlege, then so too might the future of civilization. Indeed in a world where a playwright became president of Czechoslovakia, there is hope for more humanity in our lives.

I know this speech sounds totally off-the-wall, and yet I wanted to find a different way to communicate an idea. The idea is that a new adventure always combines excitement with risk, and education, if nothing else, is an adventure. That has been my goal in teaching and working in my studio as well.

*[Speech at Art Center College of Design, Pasadena, 1990]*

# AN EVIDENT KISS

INT.- ROOM – DAY

SOUND of radio

MAN seated at a simple table in a simple chair wearing pajamas.

The rest of the room is empty.

MS Three cups of coffee appear in succession on the table.

CU cup of coffee.

MS MAN. Drinks coffee.

> MAN
>
> I wake up in a room and I don't know what to do, what to wear, whether to stand up or sit down. I know that I want a cup of steaming hot coffee. But then I never know whether to eat or not; to have bread with jam or a banana. Shall I read the newspaper while I eat. (upon reflection) I think I want a cigarette ...and some pie!

Pie and cigarette appear on table.

> MAN
>
> I like fish, but not for breakfast. I want ham and eggs. Half a pineapple

and some wheat biscuits in a basket with a checkered towel.

CU table.  Foods appear.

                              MAN
I prefer celery to cucumber, arugula to belgian endive, carrots to peas,
and squash to potato.  A large glass of wine...

White wine appears.

                              MAN
...red, not white.

Wine replaced by red. Dishes are brought to the table more and more
rapidly, replacing those already there.

                              MAN
Mmmmm....a plate of veal scallopini,  perhaps a bowl of chicken soup, a
small lemon tart, string beans, smoked salmon, peking duck, a delicious
salds of  hearts of  palm, french fried  potatoes, coquilles St. Jacques,
bouillabaise, steak au poivre, crepes suzettes, a spanish omelette, grand
marnier soufflé, graham crackers, beef stew, fricassee of chicken, roast
beef au jus, lobster tails on a bed of angel hair pasta lightly infused with
garlic, orange spice cake, tamales, ratatouille, a banana split, onion rings,
oysters rockefeller, pâté de fois gras, crème brulé, risotto milanese, a
steaming bowl of  manhattan clam chowder,  lamb chops with mint
jelly, radicchio with warm goat cheese, cauliflower au gratin, strawberry
shortcake, oh, and braised leeks.


                           FADE TO:

INT.- CAVERN - NIGHT - RED

An inverted world. Dark smokey factory space.

FIGURES of demons traverse the screen.

MAN appears crawling on the hot ground.

> MAN

What is this world? I think of ideas and then they disappear into little spirals. And there's no way in. Little Klein bottles with poisons on their surfaces. I drink from all of them. I make objects and they smother me. I write words and choke on them. I make theories and I die! Death plays the violin as I die.

SOUND of screaming duo of violins.
Flames in the cavern background.

> MAN

> (continuing)

What color are demons, the voices that whisper as you fall asleep at night and wake up in the morning. Gray for the demon of doubt. Yellow for principles. Blue-green for thinking. Black for fatigue. Red for ambition.

> DEMON 1 (O.S.)

Revulsion!! Has it come to this?

> DEMON 2 (O.S.)

You are nothing.

> MAN

I am nothing.

> DEMON 1 (O.S.)

You live through others' dreams, their theories and technologies.

> MAN

Why is everything have to be so small, fragmented, trivial, numerous, and invisible? Why can't I see anything?

DEMON 2 (O.S.)
Your theories are nothing.

CU MAN, holding up his fingers, examining them.

MAN
The tips of my fingers have sensors and yet I feel nothing.

DEMON 1 (O.S.)
To each dimension there is a finger and to each finger there are dimensions.

DEMON 2 (O.S.)
As the finger moves, so moves an entire universe tied to it by invisible strings.

DEMON 1 (O.S.)
The agents of each finger reside in the folds. Three folds on each finger hide small universes.

MAN
Nonsense! I can't exist in this world! I don't want agents. I don't want to be known. I cannot be known!

DEMON 2 (O.S.)
You have made everything. This is yours. The strings, the particles, the atoms and molecules, the numbers which make this world flow from your fingertips.
MAN

(gasping)
What??!!!

DEMON 1 (O.S.)

Yes! Five fingers, base 10. One language, base 26. One machine, base 2. One. Zero.

MAN

I want to hunt down those who would make things easy for me. The struggle is to think. I want my books. I want my own ideas. I want meaning in the clouds. I demand to see the algorithm!
MAN still crawling slowly comes upon a computer.

DEMON 1 (O.S.)

You idiot! You are back where you started You cannot escape as you walk forever on the surface of a Moebius strip!

DEMON 2 (O.S.)

What was solid transforms into fire, into vapor, into air.

MAN

I am dreaming. I know I am dreaming.

DEMON 1 (O.S)

(angered)

The last statement is a lie!
ANOTHER ANGLE.

DEMON 2 (O.S.)

While you dream your brain organizes terabytes of little details. Satisfied with its work, it reflects to itself, "Ah, this is good", and runs through the archives of memory for fun! And you just sleep through this?

DEMON 1 (O.S.)

You and your algorithm. Your lofty smoke stack puffs useless dust. Guilt racks your conscience, self-doubt gnaws at your mangled ego.

DEMON 2 (O.S.)

Detail is survival. You're dumber than a bat. At least they can find their babies in a cave of thousands of screaming voices. Can you do that?

DEMON 1 (O.S.)

A man detects passion, or a lie, in a twitch of a tiny muscle in the soft facial skin near his lover's eye. You are blind! Oh, how many times you have been betrayed!

ANGLE on MAN looking at computer.

MAN

Too many things! No! Too many ways that anything can turn into anything else! And where does it lead? To global digital democracy and a richness of expression hitherto unknown or a glut of useless diversity, a heap of digital trash, the massive trivialization of all things? I want ideas! I want a life. You have conceptualized the whole universe and it's flawless. But where are it's qualities? I don't want any part of this world! The mockery that details make of us! The lies!

MAN smashes computer, collapses.

DEMON 2 (O.S.)

Humans, as for all beings and all things, are just made of little bits. This tug of war of big ideas and tiny details is a joke!

DEMON 1 (O.S.)

Tug of war! Big ideas!

DEMON 2 (O.S.)

Detail is survival!

MUSIC, wild, then calmer. DEMON 3 appears as the MAN dressed in white suit and wide-brimmed hat.

DEMON 3
(whispering to MAN)
Your digital quandary, your quest for a formula, your conflict won't change the flow of the universe.

CU MAN looking up.

DEMON 3
(continuing)
Is there anything which is not destined for extinction as prophesied by DNA, algorithms or the cycles of civilization and time? Music, nature, the human form, god, geometry, a clock? The sand?

MS MAN animating slowly. Reaches into the surrounding sand and finds a NEWSPAPER.

DEMON 3
You'll see. You'll see...

LS DEMON 3 standing, looks down, turns to look at the mountain in the distance, walks away, backlit.

DEMON 3
(while walking)
Time meanders like the coastline of an invisible continent. It's bays are periods of repose. Its cities are the moments of creativity, and countries the map of projects. You'll see...

MS MAN turning to watch DEMON walk away.

FADE to BLACK.

*[Excerpt from the script An Evident Kiss, experimental video, 2000]*

# A SHORT RIFF ON MOBILITY

A blazing sun rises above the horizon. The evening's blanket of humidity levitates over fields of flowers like a great dirigible, and lifts off elegantly into the atmosphere, disappearing out of range and joining the diurnal flow. Radiation from the sun ignites activity in the soil. The society of microbes and the subsurface insectiary begin their daily rituals. A network of thermal, electrical and chemical sensations awakens. This metropolis is alive with motion, vibrant with industry, and this, totally invisible from the surface. Sow bugs unroll from their spherical pods, yawning, and burrow to the surface, as earthworms prepare new tunnels, explore their frontiers, seek a new definition of their universe, while entraining nitrogen in the soil, the future repast for the botanical inhabitants above, whose legs, whose vehicles of growth move steadily hungrily downward, past the buried larvæ of insects that inhabit the darkness, and past molecules whose genetic strands choreograph a sometimes stately, sometimes frenetic dance of regeneration. Travel below ground, burrowing in order to move, is a primitive state, metaphorically replicating the conditions of countries where people talk animatedly, walk relatively slowly and only dream of the possibilities of universes far away.

Meanwhile, over three-fourths of the earth's surface, rays of sunlight penetrate earnestly into water, harmonious songs of distant whales travel miles in myriad advancing oscillations. Microscopic radiolaria fabricate intricate geodesic carriage-work around their internal engines. Plankton shimmer just below the waves, sending signals skyward and casting pointillist shadows on passing seahorses. Great swarms of krill perform a microscale side stroke and the cilia of miniature cells undulate, propelling the nucleic passengers about; it is motion in search of a destination.

Other natural machines prefer the relative calm of the intersection of sky and water, atop the liquid cover of a pool, playing against the forces of surface tension, feeling the influence of the moon. The progeny of mosquitoes wriggle while their parents skate on the surface, flexing their micro-musculature against the pull.

At the earth and air interface, crawling insects inch  forward with astonishing mechanical prowess. Freed from the abominable friction and claustrophobia of the subterranean world, a centipede tracks the ground past a colony of ants who have come to the surface to eat, detected on their built in radar from a distance of one million times their body length. The ground is made for speed; the friendly horizon is a reassuring guide. Turn as you wish, circle or reverse, and the horizon holds. Transceiver-bearing insects process the equivalent of one terabyte of data every hour, joining in an "internet" of communication which unites the neighborhood in a web and which responds quickly to nourishment, sun and rain, to the protection of young offspring and to predators and makers of war. Spiders add the third dimension to the web, ascending vertical and oblique planes, doing a tightrope walk each day, casting nets upon the air, making connections, weaving filigree in amongst the molecules of the atmosphere of gases where those that fly make their way.

To take to the air is to be truly free. A dragonfly skims the a rippling pond, slaloming around a course of mosquitoes and then zooms skyward, mocking gravity, laughing as its enormous wings beat the air into vortices  which will send small flies into tumbling, screaming paroxysms of disorientation. Below, a convocation of bumblebees perform a ritual jig. Finally, a scout or two take to the air, hover, spin, rise, dive and hover again, flirting with the tantalizing seductress of a rose petal. The ether crackles with sounds, buzzings, flappings, as miniature motors rev and propellers invoke the dialogue of action and reaction, in a swirl of wave fronts and wind.

To move is also human, to fly divine. All beings in Nature are united, if not always in common purpose, then in dynamism.

Insects began the dance of motion on Earth and will in all likelihood outlive all other species that move. Insects set the paradigm of a mobile culture, of a society in perpetual animation, and every action has its context, a natural imperative. So it is that a lone vehicle has no meaning unless it is a pixel in a larger portrait of mobility. And mobility has no meaning unless its context is the entire universe.

*[Essay for Designworks/BMW, Los Angeles, 1995]*

# AND WHAT ABOUT INDUSTRIAL DESIGN?

Any attempt to grasp what is going on in industrial design these days has at some point to come to terms with two tendencies: the lure to satisfy an insatiable public craving for "entertainment" among the consuming populace and an obvious urgency to address some real problems like the environmentally conscious use of materials and a more legible human-machine interface for the operation of increasingly complex electronic products. Interestingly enough, there seems to be enough awareness and energy among most practicing designers to let these tendencies co-exist, and even begin to converge: ecological responsibility has been celebrated in form and material by some designers and is no longer relegated to a miserably utilitarian status. Likewise, most designers realize that even the most trivial or glitzy product ought to be designed for recycling and ease of use.

Nevertheless, like architects, industrial designers are at times criticized for doing their work only to please each other, ignoring users and clients needs, quixotically seeking an elusive higher plane by invoking arcane references of every conceivable kind to justify directions, styling quirks and even functions, all of which are often seen by the rest of the world as irrelevant, decadent or egomaniacal excursions. You might, at a gathering of designers, for example, overhear a conversation about the semantics appropriate for a toaster or the emotion evoked by an ear thermometer, issues of no apparent consequence to a hungry consumer who has the flu.

On the other hand, there is arguably no other field within the design professions that is so wonderfully chaotic and exuberant, that invites so diverse a group of practitioners, and that disseminates such a voluminous body of artifacts, large and small, to its clients and consumers, as does industrial design.

The conspicuous symbiosis of industrial design with commerce, advertising, need and image manifests itself in objects of manufacture that surround the lives of most of the inhabitants of developed and developing nations on earth. You'll see this in the pages of magazines at newsstands in any international airport in the world. And because the profession's design intelligence, such as it is, is brought to bear on so many common products where one design may seem to be just as good as another, there can be a freer mood, a sense of humor almost, about manufactured products, which is rarely encountered in buildings and works of fine art.

In the world of industrial design, what sells is somehow thought to be viable; if it provokes debate and piques interest in the design community, so much the better. A juicer designed by Philippe Starck may not make tastier juice, but will certainly make for tastier conversation.

The majority of industrial designers have stayed near the sidelines of philosophical debate and critical discourse, preferring to play with shape and material instead of words. Rather than intellectual neglect, this is perhaps more that industrial design's focus is scaled down, personal and immediate, object oriented, not spatial; the design of a human-sized object, a pair of glasses, a chair, and even a car, satisfies the hand as much as the brain, in appealing both to the sense of touch and a palpable pleasure of possession. The majority of designers in the mainstream, despite the phenomena of functional analyses, user testing, and engineering, are fundamentally and unabashedly motivated by a deep-seated desire to produce something which looks "cool." It is simply a part of the culture of industrial designers who are relatively free from the manifold responsibilities of the architect, to please client and contractor, to assure a level of environmental comfort and life safety, and to fit into a fixed locus a work which must serve and endure. Works of industrial design, particularly consumer products, evolve, then dwindle, more rapidly and must "sell" in a much different marketplace to a group of unknown users. Industrial design, in its relatively short history has produced a culture where cleverness and novelty as well as process and materials attract a different breed of designer from the practitioners who gravitate to the arguably more serious and lofty discourse of architecture. While architects may be looking to the muses for inspiration, to the collective architectural brain for philosophy and reason, and to the periphery of the field for career change, the industrial designer's avowed purpose is to bring visual and sensory nourishment into people's lives or to give character to an otherwise bland assemblage of machinery. Now, in a healthier economy, jobs are plentiful, consultancies are growing, and consumers are buying. Designers in this sort of environment want to roll up their sleeves, literally and metaphorically, and get their hands dirty. It is, in the late '90s, a time to work.

Even if it is true that buildings or works of fine art, owing either to a much longer tradition or to grander scale and budget, seem so magnetic intellectually, objects of manufacture nevertheless are also important signifiers of subcultures of fashion and taste, icons in the evolving aesthetic, socioeconomic, and heavily inflected language of civilization as expressed in the arts. Consider the ways in which the automobile, clothing, cellular phones and computers, even kitchen appliances, have populated the households of both urbanites and village dwellers, and how advertising has spread a fairy dust of product consciousness around the entire globe. The message of this medium is "you are what you own", and a lexicon of self-defining choices is a close as your picture tube or neighborhood magazine stand. In this cultural climate, the richness of current industrial design vocabulary permits expression much more tantalizing, poetic, accessible and amusing than the weighty historical baggage of "form follows function". Design now promises an experience, an enrichment of sorts, a kind of visual literacy and a means of the transfer of information (and, hopefully, insight) from designer to user via the proliferation of everyday objects.

Extremely diverse sources of inspiration inform the conception of recent products. New technologies seek new applications, a real design "consciousness" has awakened at last in the world of American business, the global economy is no longer a cliché but a fact of commerce, and demand for "entertainment" design in the things we buy and places we go has burgeoned. What of the creative process from which new ideas derive? Whereas past interpretations of "design as problem solving" might have served well in a functionalist world, now one could also argue that form follows idea, and that the best products these days exhibit a layered collage of influences, elements and intentions. A bamboo bicycle, an ergonomically shaped digital video camera, a pneumatic shower enclosure and even chocolates with decorative silk-screened patterns might typify these new products that have a freshness of thought and delightful surprises.

Designers in the last moments of the millennium find themselves in the most fertile, responsive territory the profession has yet known. The entrepreneur, sole practitioner, consultant and corporate designer can anticipate a brilliant future, along with the consumers of the world who await with eagerness their output. Examples presented here, drawn from the international press in the last year, provide a cornucopia of designed objects, with stories of function, material, shape, color, fashion, culture and idea.

Consider the glass water faucet designed by Arnout Visser's (from the Dutch design collective, Droog). A departure from the styling-based rehashing of form we have come to expect in many products, in Visser's design, transparent water-filled conduits, reminiscent of chemistry lab fittings, turn correspondingly blue and red, for cold and hot. Celebrating water more than plumbing, the design evolves simply from physics, not neo-neoclassic reference or arbitrary choice of a shape.

The most successful current work can be appreciated in multiple ways and derives from unexpected juxtapositions of elements. This might, for example, translate into a table by Niccolò Baldassini in which a thin square of acrylic hovers above an articulated tension structure in an elegant reversal of the conventional relationship of load and support. Innovative materials, often now justifiable ecologically, have produced some novel results as designers learn to celebrate rather than deride a more ecologically friendly world. Chairs of recycled milk containers, tableware fashioned from potato starch and office workstations made of cardboard, just to name a few "eco" products, were unimaginable only a few years ago.    Attention has also now turned to the black box, as manufacturers press designers for ways of distinguishing one stereo system or computer from another as these products compete for consumers' attention and have no inherently interesting or visible mechanical function. Even though a radio or calculator's function might be wildly dynamic at the molecular level, we are left either to admire the sculptural beauty of the enclosure, to be lulled by the soft whirring of a cooling fan, or ponder the so-called "interface", the graphical and perceptual juncture where human meets machine.

From CD-player to laboratory blood analyzer, from computer to automobile, there is scarcely a product category unaltered by digital technology. Among those products inhabited by microchips or linked by satellite and fiber optic strands, a commonality of technology points to a convergence where fax machines become scanners, entertainment system becomes workstation, "home" and "office" lose their separate identities, and where fewer products do more things. This meiosis of objects may further a  philosophical and informational convergence of all the design disciplines, and with that, a new definition of what it means "to design".

*[Published in Harvard Design Magazine, Summer 1998]*

# FOR FORTY YEARS I HAVE TRIED TO UNDERSTAND THE MOON

*An Elegy on the Death of O.K. Ervin*

PROLOGUE

For forty years I have tried to understand the moon, to master the mathematics of its motion and to read its physiognomy. I have also examined the sky to find meaning in a drop of rain, on days where there are clouds and the atmosphere is saturated with humidity. I have flown into the atmosphere and touched a cloud to try to understand.

In the rain, the sky comes alive in a flow of water. 12-billion-year-old molecules dance, redesigning themselves in the air, replicating an ancient memory of form. Follow a cloud in the sky and watch it boil, evaporate, move at the pace of the hands of a great clock. Rain falling on the surface of the ocean delineates at pattern with no direction, only a glassy surface of choice where infinite paths invite you.

In the place of the writer, where late at night cars pass on a road through the hills, the sound is like an ocean. Night follows day, the temperature lowers, there is a slight breeze, the ticking of clocks, the unconscious awaiting its moment, the arrival of dark sleep, the conscious ready to give up its hold.

In corridors, the air shimmered as molecules moved to fill the void, shimmering to account for the wound, shimmering with murmurs and the palpable ether of disbelief. That night on the phone, colleagues discussed their own mortality. Men who hadn't professed love in more than a month made love to their wives, drank and cried. A torrent of experience flowed through this wound in a single day. The conscious screamed in denial as the unconscious dealt with the flood in the natural process which closes wounds, so that by the second day, only quiet memories floated through the long white halls, 900 feet above the plane of the sea in the hills above Pasadena.

TIME

The future is an array of days on an endless string, an infinite necklace of perfect ellipses like the faces of clocks, refined by the geometry which phrases the language of things past. For each ellipse is a rectangle, a photograph, a portrait in time of a memory linked to infinity as if to form a great kite in the sky. New pictures form beyond the clouds in the darkness of the far future where the kite is propelled by the wind of dreams.

All throughout the universe, clocks are ticking, recording the formation of days and of memories. Time is the heartbeat of the universe, for without time there is no movement; without time the string of memory is broken and the rhythm of motion slows until it is gone.

Without time there is no beauty, for there can be no evolution. Without time there is no space, no cavern to contain growing and refining, no cause or effect, none of the dynamic mechanism of cosmic structure to which hungry human brains direct their instinct and awe.

How does a design take shape if not through time and space and a sequence of events deeply and universally human. This is process, and it cannot exist without time. Someone makes a sketch on a piece of paper, initiating a voyage through time and the network of cells where time, through the mechanism of memory, resides.

The phases of a life are the chapters in a book of memory where loss of innocence, creation, movement, love and birth are written. Once born, a new clock begins its ticking, its writing, its creation, its cycle.

It is possible to die on the wrong day, and we call this death untimely.

> *...in the general theory of relativity... space and time are... dynamic quantities: when a body moves, or a force acts, it affects the curvature of space and time*

*— and in turn the structure of space-time affects the way in which bodies move and forces act. Space and time not only affect, but are affected by everything that happens in the universe...This new understanding of space and time was to revolutionize our view of the universe. The old idea of an essentially unchanging universe that could have existed, and could continue to exist forever, was replaced by the notion of a dynamic expanding universe that seemed to have begun a finite time ago, and that might end at a finite time in the future...Einstein's general theory of relativity implied that the universe must have a beginning, and, possibly, an end. (Stephen Hawking 'A Brief History of Time', 1988)*

## BEAUTY

In every tree there is a beauty which the ticking of molecular clocks, the cycle of rain, and the pulsation of heavenly bodies induces, through the process of nature, which informs all things that grow, which invests form with seductive allure, and which invites all who know this to dance.

But try to capture beauty and it eludes capture, traveling on back roads where lesser themes travel less, through dense forests and at the edge of the sea.

Beauty spins, propelled by symmetry and proportion, growth and form, nostalgia and longing; longing to say, to create, to be; a smoldering furnace in the imagination.

Can it only be as deep as skin, to which we hold a mirror to see ourselves as others see us? In the mirror we measure and react; it is in the mirror that our process takes shape. In another mirror the things we make and do are also read, sometimes invoking beauty, if we can read the signs and see these things as mirrors themselves.

Beauty on the inside, a deeper one perhaps, needs new mirrors, but the x-ray and sonogram, mirrors of the interior, can't be read so fluently, only as cold diagrams of the intent to be, the intent to radiate beauty.

To see our brain and hand, look on the interior. And whereas we understand the hand, we know less about the brain and perhaps even less about the heart. What is inner beauty if not process, and process lives among molecules.

Without the heart, a brain cannot survive...is a heart itself not supremely beautiful?

> *The heart and pericardium lie in the mid-portion of the inferior mediastinum, considerably overlapped by the pleural membranes. The thin triangularis muscle overlies the pericardium in front, and between this and the costal cartilages on either side of the sternum, pass down the internal mammary arteries and veins...The heart, as seen through a fully opened pericardium, presents its right ventricle to view, a portion only of the left ventricle being barely visible. The right coronary vessels appear between ventricle and right auricle, and the visible part of the left coronary artery passes down the sulcus separating the right and left ventricle. Injury to one of the vessels by a wound is usually fatal. (John Homans, 'A Textbook of Surgery', 1936)*

DEATH

Is it a dark force of Nature, fatigue, resistance to flow, or the hearts' own curiosity, the desire to dream, to risk? Silence is a dream state for the heart. When a mechanism stops, it dies in silence: an airplane falls, but the heart crosses a line into a dream, wondering what it would be like not to hear its own beating.

A death is a gaping wound, and it is a human process to close wounds, but no wound heals completely, leaving a tiny opening through which DNA cannot pass, nor a molecule of helium, but it is a portal for cosmic rays and a portal for memory. Leaking through these tiniest of apertures from time to time you hear a song, the memories of our own fathers, the sensations of childhood, one page in a book, the musty smell of a case which once contained a violin, the cracks in the pavement in front the house where you were born and lived, the cries of our mothers.

What good is an object without its process? Dead elements, broken, abandoned, extinct, detached from the hands that made and used them. When a lamp no longer gives light, when a teacup can no longer contain tea, you feel the sadness of objects, and understand that process is a sustaining force, a pulsating artery of nourishment.

When a building dies, it leaves only its memories and materials. In its collapse, there is gentleness; in its decay, a strange elegance as it returns to base materials. So too with small objects and ideas, the work we do and the things we make are gradually erased as their process slows and time produces memory.

Death is the left-handed component of life's symmetry. Where there was life there was an invitation to metamorphose from base materials, to join a process, to acquire memory. When a designer dies, objects are now allowed their own life with a new process that spirals through new time in a double helix of memory and cosmic rays...

> *It seems, then, that an instinct is an urge inherent in organic life to restore an earlier state of things which the living entity has been obliged to abandon under the pressure of external disturbing forces...or to put it another way, the expression of the inertia inherent in organic life...Instincts are...bound to give a deceptive appearance of being forces tending toward change and progress, whilst in fact they are merely seeking to reach an ancient goal by paths alike, old and new....If we are to take it as a truth that knows no exception that everything living dies, for internal reasons becomes inorganic once again, then we shall be compelled to say that the aim of all life is death... (Sigmund Freud, 'Beyond the Pleasure Principle', 1919)*

LOVE

Lips thirst for a drink. A hand touches an object. A flame ignites the furnace of creation. Wings produce lift. Wheels roll. A swimmer glides through the water.

People who get ideas allow themselves to love. They stand on diving boards looking down at the blue water in pools, pondering their own willingness to fall. A pencil gets put to paper, a brush soaks up ink, a machine transmutes materials. A process has started and clocks measure its progress. One clock started 12 billion years ago, another when ores coalesced in the earth's mantle, another when continents formed, another when humans walked, another when roses first grew in England, another when the moon was full, another at the moment of birth, another when you heard music for the first time, another when your friend died, another when you saw the face of someone you could not forget.

Designers sit at desks wondering, dreaming, remembering, practicing, creating, patching holes in walls of worry watching for wounds. In their dance with the rest of the world, they dream of a perfect partner and of approval, but their dance is with the mechanism of life on earth and the society of memories that inhabits it. They look for their reflection in the mirror, to understand their role in the process that transmutes base materials into lively objects and which transfers information of both a technical and emotional kind, a dark deep sense of universal meaning from their minds, hands and hearts into durable materials which in some rare moments can be heard singing. This is a language asking to be understood. Its words are shape and feel, movement, proportion, grace, and some very-hard-to-say rightness of purpose... and love.

> *Essentially, a lathe is a power tool which causes work to revolve so that a tool in contact with the work moves laterally and removes metal. The control of the speed with which the workpiece revolves may be obtained with belts or through a gear arrangement. The power from a motor is transmitted to the spindle of the headstock through the belt or gears. The power also controls the lateral movement of the tool. One of the fundamental uses of a lathe is the turning of cylinders between centers. The ends of the bar must be prepared for centering with a hermaphrodite caliper. After the lathe is properly positioned, the work is caused to revolve. Very carefully the work is touched with a tool bit. Once the tool is cleared from the work, it is moved approximately .010" on the dial. (Herman Pollack, 'Manufacturing and Machine Tool Operations', 1979)*

PROCESS

Design floats in an ether of reinvention which surrounds us all. Objects and ideas disappear into history, into time, becoming obscured by clouds, only to return much later as a weather system, where, from a source, an object will vaporize, reform and move into an atmosphere of unconsciousness in which clouds evolve, when conditions allow, and fall back to earth into consciousness as if they were new, as design ideas, transformed, rediscovered, obscured, floating in time, forwards and backwards, filtered by moonlight, revealed by the sun, hidden in the clouds of memory, deconstructed and stored in other forms.

Once you find an idea, you have to let go of it; then you can chase it again, trace it, play with it, and let it find a current of air in which to soar; let its natural process, its ritual, its consciousness take over.

The ultimate human process is to create, and in the many ways in which it is possible, to give birth to strong forms and give voice to aspiration and instinct. At the same moment, there is a force which craves the reduction of all things to base materials, seeking sources of healthy rich fuel for creation in that which has been already long ago created; to restart clocks, to maintain the steady rhythm of a heartbeat, to make noise to fill silences.

In a creative life, two roads intertwine, conscious and unconscious, juxtaposed, symmetrical, balanced, yet composed of paths of different qualities. If the conscious one is straight, then the unconscious curves out of sight of its destination, yet leading there all the same.

A white piece of paper contains the manifestation of all ideas past in its memory, ready to be released from darkness, to have its many hidden forms traced, to become a record of process, to become a new map, a map of the human nervous system, a diagram of emotion and knowledge, an extension of the human being: the designer.

Like the rain which fall from the sky into the vessel of the oceans on earth, and like the water in oceans which rises to the sky to make rain, so it is that the highest efforts of man, the deepest motivations, the love of life that designers put into their work, that artists put into their paintings, sculptors into stone, writers into words, all these flow into a great vessel of human expression, full of memory and wisdom, fear and complexity, sound and light, form and idea, photographs and whispers. Our ancestors, our teachers, those whom we love, have contributed to the vessel into which we have contributed our work and from which our contributions, and our souls, are taken and reformed.

Under a new moon, ideas grow. A new life is about to begin.

*[Narration for video, screened at Art Center College of Design, Pasadena, and the Industrial Designers Society National Conference, Orlando, 1996]*

# TOAST IN ONE-SYLLABLE WORDS FOR TIM BUTTE

She said I should make a toast for you, Tim.
And I said YES and then I thought
Oh, Boy, I need a thought!
What should I say?
And so I thought of toasts of the old days with words like wine and mead and beer and brew......and skøl. Words used by men who wore hats with horns; not words from Rome, oh no, but short words from Eire and the Isles in the North Sea where great short words came from to our own tongue!

So I made some strict rules and wrote a long verse to make a toast with none but short words... and it is quite weird. And I call it "There Are Things You Just Can't Say".

Oh Butte, Oh Tim Butte,
You who were taught to love trees,
And save trees...
(You see what I mean about the rule to use none but short words?)
Oh friend, oh fine man with a short name!
You go and we cry!
You came to this place,
This big black Art School
With your black car
To help get bucks for art
So kids who come here can learn,

And get fame and then get their own bucks and big new cars and a nice place to live.

Thanks for all you did to help, Old Friend. Thanks to your Mom and Dad, who made you and gave you two short names so I could write this toast!

You have a big heart and a fine head. With these and your short names and your great fame, you get to have a verse like this when you go, long in length but short in word.

But then I think: Why did we not say this while you were still here, or did we?

I guess there are just things you can't say.

Do you know how much these guys and gals will miss you? Those who teach and those who learn and those who say things and those who hear? All of them will miss you when you go. And do you know that they all thought you were great?

Then there were those guys from the world of bucks who brought some of those bucks here. They thought you were great too!

At night we saw you here late; through the glass you could be seen in your place, at your desk, on the phone, deep in thought. We knew it was great that you work so much; by day and by night we saw you there, with your notes and that pile of stuff on your desk, getting bucks for art. We saw you there when we went to our cars and thought in our heads "What a guy, what a great guy. He is fine and we like him too much!"

And we know we need him. Did we say that when you were here, Tim? Did you hear it? Why did we have to wait for now? So I say it now, oh great guy: You go and we cry!

We do not like to say it, but we know this will be good for you and fun to have a new life... to put your black car with the name like a horse in a new space, not in the lot out back of this Art School but a new place where they need you too.

Bring more bucks and fame to those who need these things. And we hope that those new guys know how great you are. Tell those new guys that all of the guys and gals here miss you.

And may those new guys give YOU bucks, more bucks than here, since he who got bucks for an Art School, like you did, is a saint with a brain and heart, and a saint who goes to get bucks, needs bucks!

Let us now toast you and give thanks! Not from the top of our hearts, but from the place in our hearts that you all know.

Let us now raise a glass high, the way they did in days gone by and try to say the things that are hard to say:

You go, we cry... but not for long, since we will still be friends; and joke and laugh and talk by phone, and use the fax for a long, long time.

Tim Butte, thanks!
Thanks for what you did here...
...and thanks for who you are!
This is not the end, old pal.
This is just the start!


*[Farewell speech at Art Center College of Design for the Director of Corporate Relations, Pasadena 1997]*

# ODE TO AN EARN OR HEY!

When in the horse of human events
It becomes necessary to go,
To move at a gallop,
To give a wallop on the hind quarters,
To jockey into a new position,
To find a bay for repose,
To not rest, least of all on a laurel.

When your figure is full,
The sheet in balance,
When donors donne or,
And you dun 'em all,
And you done all you can,
Giving is dunne, John.
It ain't.  Hey!!

Ivory, ebony, telephony.
From a figured base,
The coin of the realm was trebled at an interesting rate
Without ritard, now a fugal state
Pushes toward a kind of code, ah!
No discord ever, harmony is key. see?
Dough?  Fah!!!
Does this fall flat on deaf ears?
Whoa!

What's an ode without a rhyme,
An equine mouth without effluvial slime,
A Viennese waltz in 7/8 time,
A fiduciary note with a rate not prime,
A Perrier without a lime,
A kosher pickle without the brine?
A Pepto without Bismol, a Wrap without Saran?
The sound of clapping with only one han',
Beethoven minus Ludwig Van?
The show without the pan,
Art Center College without Dyan?

Pianissimo, no forte!
Upright, no grand!
She's in the saddle astride middle C
On a grid of ledger lines and spaces.
And what a staff!
The dulcet tones which make a chorus.
How she held the reins around a track record.
Sometimes sulky, but always sharp.
Like a melody, unforgetable!
Classical.

As refined as a Grecian vessel or a Roman verse, as Ovid said:
"In all creation no thing endures, all is in endless flux, each wandering
shape a pilgrim passing by. As wave is driven by wave and each, pursued,
pursues the wave ahead, so time flies on and follows, flies and follows,
always, forever new. What was before is left behind, what never was is
now, and every passing moment is renewed."

So, you see, little filly?
It's not really a finale,
The mane thing is that life is a succession of TASTY BUNDLEs *
An epic poem with verses in a different rhyme,
Tunes in different keys.

Take note then.
There's a gift horse over there playing the piano.
Giddyup, what are you waiting for?
There's a lot  more music after this...


*[Farewell speech for Dyan Sublett, Sr. VP of Development,  Art Center College of  Design, 2000]*


*[\* an anagram on Dyan Sublett]*

# INSIDE

It is late at night and my Audi A2 is parked under a street lamp, svelte, iridescent and perfectly proportioned. This car puzzles and disturbs some people while others lump it into the category of other such vehicles, but in my opinion, as a form, it stands alone among recent automobiles, if only for its exterior good looks. It is entertaining and wonderful to activate the little remote control transmitter that unlocks the car, just to see the interior begin to glow in the darkness from afar. It is as if a light has been illuminated in the window as a warm welcome. The open door invites entry. Once inside, you feel at home.

My A2 follows my preferences through a lineage of automobiles from an Austin Healy, Citroen DS and Volvo P1800 to a modest, clever Honda CRX. It was of course, the Citroen, one of the most elegant and innovative cars ever built, that taught me about interior space. Having driven a variety of cars, I used to appreciate the feeling of an enveloping cocoon and a recumbent posture. But now I am happier sitting more vertically, as if at a table. And with adequate headroom and adequate distance to the glass. And without massive protuberances or techno-graphically ostentatious displays. I want it simple and clean. I want habitable space, and the interior of the A2 provides just that. This is, after all, my "workplace". And I want it to be just right!

In the history of mobility, no vehicle has been as enclosed, distanced from the outside world as the modern automobile, sealed against the wind and smell, cushioned from excessive vibration or shielded from the sun as current models. It is a very different experience from the back of a camel, the flatbed of a wagon or the open cockpit of an old biplane. The modern car has become a room. With a view of the outside and the isolation of effectively being indoors, you have only to guide this room from A to B safely and without getting lost. It is precisely this eerie distancing that makes the interior of a car such an excellent mind space. It is perhaps second only to a bed as a laboratory of the imagination.

The interior of a car is for me not a cockpit, although I have been through that phase in the past. But once having flown real airplanes with real cockpits, the simulation in a car becomes a poor substitute, even as a fantasy. Now I must say that I appreciate the automotive interior more as a conceptual place, ideally as unburdened by technological manifestations of control as possible. It's the view I want, a view of a skyline or landscape in dynamic perspective. That, plus some time to appreciate this. And to think.

I get some of my best ideas in the car. It is an encapsulated chamber, sort of like a steamy hot shower. The hum of tires on the pavement and the images on the "movie screen" of the windshield must certainly generate calming and beneficial alpha waves in the brain, just like the restful sound of running water or the sound of a flute. I have also had some productive meetings in the car, hatched new ideas with collaborators, made deals and had some romantic arguments; granted some of these might well have taken place in my apartment, but not all of them. Despite being a "personal space", the car interior is relatively anonymous, a manufactured product after all, so the crossing of territorial boundaries of home, work and office is not an issue and the space is deliciously neutral in a way. Doesn't everyone know what to expect from the inside of a car? The added benefit of a car is that this little environment is mobile, so at the end of a heated discussion, a conceptual breakthrough, a lover's quarrel or just a pleasant conversation, there can be a cup coffee or a beautiful view or the diversion of rush hour traffic at the conclusion!

There are two ways to think about driving. The more obvious is the dynamic process of interaction of human and machine, the active monitoring of the parameters of motion and road conditions, the smooth shifting of gears for acceleration and the judicious application of brakes to bring the vehicle to a stop. But the other way to look at driving is offered by professional pilots who describe flying as long periods of numbing boredom punctuated only rarely by seconds of sheer terror! Put another way, to drive is to sit down, wait and stand up! It is much the same in a living room at the end of the day, sitting in a comfortable chair with a glass of wine listening to music. It is only in an emergency that sudden dynamic response is necessary. Either you are about to crash into another car, or the house has caught fire, for example! The common situation of two people sitting side by side at home on a sofa watching television or conversing, is not much different from sitting in a car on a highway contemplating the scenery or having a talk. At home you can go to the refrigerator for a beer during an advertising break, whereas in a car you can stop by the side of the road for a sandwich.

Suddenly a grand unification theory of the commonality of domestic and automotive interior activity seems to be emerging. If you accept the premise of the car as a mobile extension of home, then the only obvious flaw seems to be that in most cars you can't walk around. Or hang pictures on the wall. But I have seen some combi vans where you can do both! In the end is there any difference between driving a car and sitting at the kitchen table working at the computer or reading a good book?!

I have just changed apartments in the building in which I live, to a living unit which is the mirror image of the previous one. It is as disorienting as it is familiar and this shows the important relationship that furniture, windows, door swings and handles have to everyday life in a room. I have stumbled through the experience for several days and have only just begun to come to terms with this left-handed, flipped world. I had found in the first apartment a comfortable place at the end of the kitchen table where I liked to write, with my left side to the wall. It was in fact the same position as my driving position, with right hand on the wheel and left arm on the sill of the open window on a warm sunny day. But now I feel like a passenger. I am sitting at an identical kitchen table, facing my computer screen, but the window is now on my right. And someone else is at the wheel. To experience

this fresh and curious sensation, get a friend to drive your car as you
sit in the passenger seat. To be sure, we arrange furniture in our living
spaces to suit an interesting variety of needs, not the least of which
is composition, a sort of aesthetic condition like the balanced repose
of Japanese "kanji", not one of which is strictly symmetrical. We also
arrange furniture for comfort and function, we orient certain places to
a view, a fireplace or a television screen, for example, all to satisfy the
human perceptual apparatus that makes us feel "at home" in space. In
cars, however, we are seated in a theatre, watching the drama of motion
side-by-side with our companions, and with all the other drivers and
passengers in cars that happen to be going in the same direction on the
road.

There is a very good reason that cars generally follow a traditional
layout of interior parts, so that the knowledge of operation is
transferable from driver to driver and from car to car. This of course
leaves car designers at the mercy of a limited space in which to work, let
alone innovate. So the matter of design becomes a matter of details and
styling that has resulted in solutions both elegant and goofy, clusters of
instruments and controls that look like a spaceship or the front of an
old pipe organ. There is a very special architecture of this cockpit, and a
special design language that has taken most of its cues from computers,
airplane flight decks, or car styling of the past.

This said, it is fascinating to note that traditional interiors follow the
same logic. Standard elements arranged in traditional layouts, narrow the
vocabulary of the interior designer to the details of colors, shapes and
finishes, which also has ended up with rooms beautiful, kitchy or absurd.
Yet we want normalcy and a certain amount of classic organization. We
expect the interior of a room to be populated with chairs and tables,
with windows and doors, with bookcases and cabinets, and with an
occasional stairway or grand piano. The standard elements are thus
welcome; no users manual necessary! The known identity of room and
car leaves us gratefully unchallenged; it is nice to sit down in comfort
facing the view of a garden or a road, and to have a friend nearby in a
position conducive to talking. So, yes, the chair, the table, the window
and bookcase form the familiar interior environment, just as the chair,

table, window and cabinet compose the car interior, only we refer to these things as seat, dashboard, windshield and glove box.

And there on the table are placemats, dishes and silverware defining a place to sit down and eat. Once taught as children the symbols of a civilized domestic life, we never forget in which hand to hold the fork and knife and where to expect a glass of water. It's as automatic as reaching for the ignition, using the turn signal, and keeping both hands on the wheel.

The shape of car furniture has reached a particularly high peak, which in one regard has surpassed its residential cousins. And that is adaptability. Of course, it is possible to sleep on a couch or rest one's elbows on a table, but the car seat is a marvel of adjustability and multifunction, in the name of ergonomics, safety and sport. But isn't it really a throne? One can sit erect or rule the mobile domain with ease. It is all about position, not only of the body, but also of status for some people who show off their machines and derive a sense of identity from a certain mark, and position in space. The seat is the apparatus of spatial comfort, imagination and the sense of repose that makes driving such a cerebral and effortless experience.

As you might expect, I have the same expectations of my living space that I do for my car. Simplicity and space. Not large, but generous and open, a good place for the human spirit to inhabit. To experience this space fully, I prefer to drive with the seat pushed as far back as it will comfortably go. It is the position of a person in a room, or at least a person sitting at a table with the chair pushed back. The interior of the A2 supplies a great deal of comfort in this position, as well as presenting a broad, flat horizon of a dashboard, like a black sandy beach, and a broadly curved ceiling and glass like the canopy of the night sky.

The feeling of interior space aside, an environment is also the sum of its surfaces, volumes, details and subtleties. It is here that the language of design defines the character and quality of an interior experience. The A2 provides this character without resorting to lavish materials. This is a character of form. Just look at the center console, tall and unconventional, more like a cabinet than a dashboard, more furniture than sculpture. There is no pretense here, just legibility: things work the way they should and everything you need is within reach. Couple this with the upright posture of the seats and the excellent view through the windows and you have a domestic interior experience much like a room.

I don't like to decorate the space I live in. And I don't really like a room decorated by others. Or a car for that matter. Maybe I'm a typical minimalist architect or perhaps I'm just crazy, but I really appreciate the "inner beauty" of an unornamented spatial world without the burden of having to my mark my territory with decoration. It's how I like to live. And drive.

*[Published in Slovene as "Avtodom" in Ambient, Ljubljana, July 2003]*

# TWO LOVES AT FIRST SIGHT

I have a confession to make. Well, two confessions actually. I have fallen in love. Twice. It's irrational, but you know the symptoms. A short breath, the almost imperceptible gasp of air and recognition, and the knot in your stomach as desire invades your psyche.

You see her under the light of a full moon in winter. She does not reveal herself much at the beginning. Is it modesty or just the hint of colors beneath the gauzy filter of a snowfall? Here and there a glimpse of what's possible, moments of her beauty. She wears a necklace of light, yet her charms are distant. You're surprised to hear words whispered in your ear in a strange language. They fly past like birds racing on the wind. The moonlight flatters her. It will never be like this the second time.

It took nearly a year to find her again. I feel as though I can say that I live in her heart. I call her "beloved" and I feel somehow she has been named this before. Inopportunely perhaps, another love catches my peripheral vision, a blur in motion like the first, but this one flirts openly. She's witty. Irresistible. I want her.

"Ljubljana" names one love. The other is known cryptically as "A2". I invent the first awkward conversation:

ME: *Come here often?*
A2: *No. Not as much as I would like.*
ME: *Want to go for a ride?*
A2: *I hardly know you.*

And that's how it started; the attention was all she needed! She wrapped herself around me like a glove. I felt her purring as the wind blew more strongly. Her curves entranced me; the cool feel of her skin thrilled the touch. She turned heads in Italy. They wondered, "Who is that?" They want to drive her. You desperately crave a peak under her skirt and yet she only reveals her assets through a narrow window. With her permission you remove the cover. It's like a giant feather in your hands. And underneath, the satiny mechanism glistens.

You can love a city or a country. And you can love a car. And where does love come from if not some strange chemistry, some dynamic of thought and feeling inspired by beauty. Fortunately, we are not all alike. We only respond magnetically when a certain form attracts us, like the shoes that transport us, the skin we touch, or the voice speaking our language. To open the door of a car for the first time is to cross the border to an unfamiliar land. To know an automobile is to know a city and its landscape: its scent and feel, its architecture and customs, and where the soft, smart, dolphin-like faces of the people greet you with welcome.

Apparently, I speak A2. And not since the '80s, when I owned an irresistibly elegant and wacky 1972 Citroen DS (La Déesse!), have I heard such a lyrical voice of intelligible design language, and experienced the hand of a skilled creator at work.

| Ljubljana | A2 |
| --- | --- |
| Small and beautiful | Small and beautiful |
| 300,000 pop. | 1400cc/3cyl. |
| 4k inhabitants/km2 | 6 l./100km |
| 10.4km (N-S) | 3826mm (length) |
| 7km (E-W) | 1462mm (wheelbase) |
| Affordable | Economical |
| Krizanke Open Air Theater | 'Open Sky' sunroof |
| Julian Alps and Karst | Front and side airbags |
| Granite | Aluminum |
| Jewel of Slovenia | Pride and joy of the family of Audi |
| Slavic, yet quietly European | Audi, yet a little bit shy |
| Charming, wired, intellectual | Hip, cool and savvy |
| Best Kept Secret in Europe | Best Kept Secret in Europe |

OK. I plead guilty to a brief affair with an Audi A4, but it wasn't true love. I also admit that I flirted with the sprightly and modestly efficient A3 and lusted unabashedly after the gorgeous A6 owned by my friend. And I can barely imagine the feeling of driving the A8. I had better stay away! Luckily, I know that the A2 feels a kinship for her biggest sister; they share the mystery and grace of the metal with which they are made. And while the company that made them has been rigorous about assigning a generous amount of Audi look and feel to each of their offspring, I secretly harbor the notion that the A2 and the A8 got extra attention. It is well known that beauty and intelligence in families tend to skip generations and that not all 5 sisters will be equally well endowed. The eldest is a leader with dignity, while the little sister will go "off-road" to find her own way.

I ask myself: Is it better to have two loves to be able to compare, to deepen understanding, to choose, to contrast one's charms with the other's?

A friend of mine calls this country the "little giant" and the same could be said for the A2. You can enter both Ljubljana, let's say, or the A2 and marvel at how so much architecture and detail of design can be accommodated in such a compact container. Attribute this to the genius of Audi designers and engineers if you like, but I would prefer to think of this more conceptually. The matter of size disappears entirely as you realize it is a character, not dimension that determines reward and that shapes satisfaction.

You get to now the A2 like you get to know a woman, layer-by-layer, fact-by-fact and feeling-by-feeling. But you also know that here is a pony that wants to gallop in the Alps. Despite her diminuitive size and her feisty 3-cylinder power plant, she goes where you lead her and she'll do anything to pass! She's quick and self-assured. The precise shifter lets you move through the gears with two fingers, if you want, as you admire the scenery on a beautiful fall day. But the precision obtains in more aggressive moves with sporty abandon as her otherwise demure face turns bolder in the rearview mirror of other cars as you position yourself to overtake slower traffic. She'll turn in a circle much tighter than most of her smaller competitors and maneuver with astonishing agility in town. Her svelte body is why! Nevertheless, as with any sassy female, her inner beauty outshines her technicalities. She seats you in safety and comfort and places the parts you touch and control very naturally and deftly. She's an Audi, all right! Surefooted, elegant, lean, responsive and cool.

Mr. Frenk Tavcar, manager of Audi here calls Slovenia "Audi Country". He beams with pride about Audi sales in this receptive country, but he also bemoans the small slice taken by the A2. It is a situation that ought to change. As the talk in Ljubljana's cafes turns to culture and as Slovenes search identity in an expanding role in Europe, eventually the intelligence that infuses this wonderful place will turn the conversation to matters of smart transportation. The A2 will be a natural consequence of those thoughts. And those of us who live and love here will smile knowingly. She is a car for the best of us. She is a car for Slovenia.

[Published as "Dve ljubezni v prvi pogled / Two Loves at First Sight", Adria Airways InFlight Magazine, Ljubljana, 2003]

# A MESSAGE IN A BOTTLE

It is a cool, clear Friday morning, on the cusp of summer-fall and the exodus is in full mobilization already. Students populate the five tendrils that lead from the city, at the five major intersections with the ring. They are easily recognizable, icons cast from a single mold, jeans, rucksacks and the requisite tags, MB, GO, and KR, among others. Later in the day, the traffic along these same pathways will increase, as the parade of automobiles joins the emigration. It is a drama played out here every week and beneath the surface of human beings in motion appears a deeper, neurobiological process of the migration of neurons in a collective brain: the tagged young ones to the warm hearth of home and the encapsulated cells in cars to nature, the mountains, the farmland and the seaside. The concentrated brain activity during the week decrescendos towards sleep as the synapses of the weekend start their dance in the provinces. And in a couple of days the pulsation reverses; the cars know their way along the dendrites back to the city; it is imbedded in their psyches, and the tags are coded with LJ on the other side.

I am the resident of a different land, waiting for insights and inspiration from the muse, material to understand where I am, for a note to put in a bottle, to send a message across the sea from the edge of the Adriatic at Piran, to explain this special place. I want it to ride the current far, to Venice, Crete, or Istanbul. My muse is laughing now and sings to me a few lyrics from a curious song of the '50s: "Istanbul was Constantinople / Now it's Istanbul not Constantinople / Been a long time gone..." She's as perceptive as she is beautiful! She's right, I think to myself as I contemplate Ljubljana ("Ljubljana, not Emona, been a long time gone...") and try to comprehend the Slovene culture below the surface, the stalactites and stalagmites of her soul.

In the tradition here, to which I am becoming all too accustomed, it is best not to cogitate on an empty stomach, since deep issues require energy and certain conviviality. I transfer my thought process therefore to a restaurant in a shopping center in Vi□, not far from where I live. I am at a table eating a salad, and I feel the suspicious glances of others on me. For Slovenes, the salad inhabits a sacred sphere, a partaking of the great bounty of Nature, a way of bringing the spirit of the land into close contact with the spirit of the body. Internally. Here you can imagine the atoms and molecules, vitamins and minerals mixing and transmuting, commingling with digestive enzymes and glorifying the exchange of particles of information that govern the universe. The same can be said of wine, whose process of creation is a direct conduit to the sun, through fruit, soil and the hands of human beings. The razorblade sourness and ruby lightness of Teran, for example, must evoke the character of Nature in the human body much as succulent juice does rushing through the veins of blood oranges.

A bowl of salad, then, is the first in a series of strange iconographies, which speak to the Slovene collective brain that I witnessed at the edge of the autocesta ring, a "state of mind", so to speak, like 2 million neurons united in language and experience and evolved to preserve itself, its identity and function. Ljubljana is the corpus callosum and frontal lobe for vital and intellectual function, with its organic pentagram of pathways of connection, to Trieste, Klagenfurt, Vienna, Zagreb and Maribor, a sort of starfish floating at the center of the unconscious; the cities and towns, and the 252 registered museums which are the repositories of collective history, come together as the regions of the cerebrum managing sensation, memory and speech, while the farmland aggregates into a medulla oblongata at the base of the brain, the so-called "lizard brain", the ancient instinct of preservation of the species, the green dragon.

But let's start at the top, with the godfather, Triglav. It is said that it is traditional for every Slovene to climb this mountain at least once in a lifetime, and therefore it must also be said that the spirit of Triglav infuses the soul of each inhabitant, as well as claiming its territory on the national flag. Triglav, with its three heads, is the ultimate "vrh" of the land, a holy trinity, "a visible expression of the Universe, personified as god of the sky, the earth, and the underworld" as I read somewhere. In the symbolic world, almost any interpretation is possible, like Food, Drink and Conversation, or Nature, Home and Country. I would think the trinity will soon begin to transmute in modern terms as World, Culture and Self, especially now when the Slovene collective brain is about to take an official role among other thinking entities in a political and economic and social capacity.

In spring, rising temperatures make the Julian Alps, and among them the three-headed godfather, emerge from hibernation and drops of sweat begin to feed the rivers, the holy trinity of the waters: the Soca, emerald green pride and joy of the country and of Nature; the Sava, the most adventurous of the three, making its way to as far as Beograd where it joins the Duna; and the Ljubljanica which winds to the eponymous capital to become its "stream of unconsciousness", a geographical and historical thread, meandering like a serpent, the green dragon diving twice underground through the mysterious karst into Italy, searching and making her place in the earth.

She is not like other mighty waterways that bisect and define Prague or Budapest, Paris or London. This river is not the spine of the city in urban terms, but instead she is a nerve, which energizes the center and weaves her memories into the matrix of the city and country. She is exotic, subtle and coquettish, mighty in her own way perhaps, but vulnerable. Her current is changeable from wild to twitchy to limpid. She is one of the leading ladies, if not the grand diva, of Ljubljana's operatic cast of characters.

She flowed here when the barje was flooded and when pole houses sheltered the dwellers of pre-history. She has offered up Roman artifacts from the treasure house of her murky bottom. And she swallowed Urska, the virgin who dared to dance with the water-man. The Ljubljanica now owns the virgin soul and in the shadow of weeping willows, the watery spirit of the insouciant, naïve and ravishing maiden laps at the river banks as the vapors of that same spirit caress the vines on Secessionist facades and mix with the Ljubljana mist. Like all mythic spirits, she did not die; she was transformed; she is very much alive.

Plecnik must have loved her dearly to have enhanced her curves with architecture and to have made not one bridge but three with which not only to cross but also to admire her.

Technically, Plecnik authored the addition of two bridges, but in so doing he composed, ironically, yet another Slovene holy trinity, this triple bridge, an icon of uncertain choices perhaps. Or an uneasy connection between church and state, centering more or less on axis from the portico of the old city hall and the steps of the luminous Fransiscan church. Or the symbolic message brought down to earth from Triglav of a tripartite character (alpinist, farmer, virgin) of the Slovenian people. Crossing a river such as this one, in this place, cannot help but meld heart, mind and soul, although here, each is a path taken one at a time.

If the Ljubljanica is the green dragon, snaking its way through holes in the land and the unconscious of Slovenes, then this dragon is not alone: the "other" dragon is the Roman Wall. Plecnik must have realized this as his reconstruction of the ruined structure provided certain zoomorphic embellishments. What was once the side of a rectangular fortified enclosure now, with Plecnik as the conduit of mythology and ritual geometry, takes on a crocodilian form, sleeping at the edge of old Emona as if it were a pond, with its arched eye scanning the landscape for activity, but allowing climbers various perches on the ordered bumps of its craggy back. Each outcropping of the crocodile's dorsal topography contains sensors, which can detect very small disturbances in the surface of water, the hints of potential prey. And so it might be that the wall knows it is being climbed. Eventually, will the sleeping lizard awaken and move? Will the tremors precipitate the changing face of Ljubljana much as the great earthquake did in 1895? In any event, the wall is not totally inert. If nothing else, the memory of Rome may still reside in its bones.

At any moment on any given day, a small percentage of the city population can be found in motion along the 33-kilometer-long pedestrian path, which rings the city, the pot, the path of memories. This Ljubljana walk meanders through parks, open land, industrial zones and over a large hill as it traces the line of an ignominious period of war and suffering. Trees and gravel have replaced barbed wire and markers stand like sentinels marking stopping points along the way. In late afternoon the path becomes more crowded, more so on Sundays, until early May when thousands join in a ceremonial circumnavigation. It will be a while before the generations who experienced the real meaning of this circle will be gone and the significance fades as the individual memories of the times must surely also fade. The beauty and uniqueness of this path, aside from the trees, the recreational opportunity and the variety of terrain, is its porosity, its many intersections with streets and other minor paths, parking lots and bridges, its openness to joining up for a short while, or leaving at any point. It is like a compass and an instrument of orientation on the plane of the earth and with respect to the many "places" and neighborhoods of Ljubljana, in addition to the cardinal points of magnetic direction. It is a major feature of the city, but its presence is announced "Ljubljana-style": quietly.

Ironically perhaps, the aerial view of the city reveals a second, concentric "path", the ring highway, and yet these two circles are sisters of very different personalities apart from the obvious point that the ring is for motor vehicles. While the pot is a path of engagement with history and nature, the road is a circle of convenience and detachment. In a sense, it is a shame that a car, for example on its way from Venice to Bratislava or from Salzburg to Sarajevo will miss the experience of Ljubljana completely. One would hope that at least signage would address the rich contents within the ring. One would also hope that the pot would become a lasting museum of memory, with a deeper contact with the past.

A circle is a chance to revisit the same points over and over again with a sense of the continuity of beginning and end. But there must be openings. Closed circles make islands of the territory they enclose.

There is another much larger circle in Slovenia—its own border—a circle, which is about to open in a way it has never done before. Yes, invasion, politics, war from outside these borders have shaped the history of this country and it is a marvel that the heart of Slovenia still beats and that its soul remains remarkably intact within its boundaries. But now, at the invitation of its European neighbors present and future, Slovenia takes its place within a larger world. The cornucopia of Slovenia is bountiful and its fruits will be tasted by many. Likewise, Slovene citizens will become citizens of Europe and go beyond the circle to partake of the riches of the outside world.

Cultural DNA will mingle with others and weave new identities from the genetic material of memory. And what of the dragon now? The virgin and the Roman wall? What of the family portrait of symbology? Slovenia, don't take too quickly from other countries, but let there be a new passion for the treasures of this country, and help set a standard of leadership in education and culture to advance the European way of life. It is the way the circle should open.

In the meantime, another player in the Slovene cast of mythological characters stands in a meadow covered with snow, waiting for the right moment to exorcise the demon of winter and welcome the exuberance of spring. He is the kurent: angel and devil in one, the "bad boy" of the fields, Bacchus, the expansive spirit who threatens a boundary rather than respects it. No border can contain this spiral phantom; he is a circle unwound, he will just leap over the fence!

To celebrate the kurent is to awaken the drives that live in every being. This spirit demands confidence and thrives on a diet of renewal and change. His long scarlet tongue wraps around the grapes that will soon become wine flowing through intestines to mingle with corpuscles and lubricate synaptic pathways. The horned demon slithers through the wild heritage of time and space, drunk with paradox, mocking destiny. He is a muse in disguise. The kurent is a mask; behind the mask is you.

A kurent also stands in the exact center of Ljubljana astride the monument to Preseren, favorite poet and cultural hero, whose soft countenance gazes quizzically at passers-by. He waits for drop of nectar from the hand of the muse, for a verse to materialize. And materialize it does:

"Prijatli! obrodile / so trte vince nam sladkó / ki nam oživlja žile /

srce razjásni in oko / ki utopi vse skrbi / v potrtih prsih up budi! The vintage, friends, is over / And here sweet wine makes, once again / Sad eyes and hearts recover / Puts fire into every vein / Drowns dull care / Everywhere / And summons hope out of despair." *

And so I compose my message:

> *To whomever finds this: I live in Ljubljana, at 46 degrees north latitude in the center of the small country of Slovenia. Some visitors thought this city reminded them of Prague. But people here know different! One has only to think of the skylines of the two cities to understand why. Prague's towers, roofs and cupolas assault the sky like missiles ready to belch fire and pierce the atmosphere, whereas Ljubljana inhabits its valley like a carpet above which hover apparitions in the moist cloud of its ubiquitous and gentle fog.*

Now a bottle floats in the Adriatic. The current takes its natural course, slowly and irrevocably.

*[Published in Delo newspaper, Saturday Supplement, 27 September, Ljubljana, 2003]*

*[* Zdravljica / A Toast, France Preseren]*

# AN ARGUMENT AGAINST CHEAP

No one can resist a good deal. Cheap prices, incentives and bargains swarm around the heads of all consumers in "civilized" societies like bumblebees and fireflies. The old idea of "You get what you pay for" just doesn't seem to work any more. We are so easily seduced and so readily addicted.

Business has come up with this idea of "value added", which tries to show that additional features of a product ought to cost more and that paying for them is worth it, both at the top and the bottom of the product line. Well, there's a darker corollary of "value removed", when a product or service falls below a certain quality or standard and when people are still urged to buy because the thing is cheap. I cringe when I hear the word "cheap" anyway, because it carries with it much more than the idea of low price and instead substitutes the pejorative ugliness of the bottom of the heap. If you want to scare yourself, look up "cheap" in the dictionary: along with the definition "charging low prices but offering good value" is "dishonorable, offensive or unfair, especially in a way that seems obvious or calculated", "worth little, or accorded little value, not deserving of respect" As if we didn't somehow know this already!

How many times have you read about mobile phones or other consumer electronics, or cars even, where the base model is really the same as the expensive models, same chip or same engine, where the amenities which are built-in in the first place (economies of scale) are then disabled or stripped away. The idea is that consumers without deep pockets can start at the bottom (entry-level) and work their way up.

These are the sorts of thoughts one gets while watching television or while waiting for an airplane. For me, recently, it was the latter, pacing around the lounge at Brnik, waiting for my flight to London to arrive. Two hours late, an orange and white bird landed on the tarmac, its name in the form of a web address screaming from fuselage, tail and nacelle. Finally on board and in the air, inflight magazines are handed out since the seatbacks don't have pouches for reading material! Seats don't recline, but you CAN buy an expensive cup of coffee.

You arrive in Stanstead where in order to catch a connecting flight, which has by now departed, you have to pass through passport control, exit and reenter as there is no transit area. Purpose of your stay in London? To get out of there as quickly as your next flight will allow. And even if you arrived more or less on time, if it's less than 40 minutes before your flight, the gate is closed and you must rebook, for a not-so-small fee, of course. And when the next flight happens to be at 6:30 in the morning, you face the unnerving prospect of sleeping in the airport or getting a hotel. And the surcharges start to add up as you book at the reservations desk, get a taxi and end up in somewhere in rural surroundings at an inn, charmingly renovated, but with creaky old beams and walls surrounding a tiny, not so inexpensive room, with a loud group of students occupying the top floor above you and partying all night. Other guests shouted expletives into the night at the front desk. It didn't work. After one hours'sleep, you get up at 4 AM to make trip back to the airport to stand in line with your eyes still shut for check in (and not a reserved seat).

I arrive in Oslo via a second cheap airline, only to find I am in a remote airport over 100 kilometers from the center. There is no currency exchange desk here, so I take a wad of Norwegian kroners from a bankomat. By now I am late for the conference I am supposed to attend and find out that an "express" bus will arrive in 45 minutes for the nearly two-hour ride to my hotel. I opt for a taxi, knowing it is expensive and spend the whole ride thinking to myself "never again", like some of the angry passengers at both airlines counters in London, like the German businessman or the UK tourist, screaming at the poor employees about the policies and service. I also try to find a moment of clarity to find out just how expensive this taxi trip will be. I convert kroners to euros over and over in my sleepy head with a different answer each time. By the time I reach my destination, I realize I have spent 200 euro on the taxi and 150 euro in London in rebooking fees and the "hotel adventure". Ironically, I arrive exactly at noon for the start of the conference. What started as an inexpensive trip ended up costing more than an ordinary ticket would have been! Expensive cost, cheap experience.

Of course, the return trip was uneventful. It's just that the inside of one plane looks like MacDonalds, oozing yellow plastic like cheap mustard, menus pasted overhead; the other plane's exterior is as offensive visually as this one is on the inside, likewise the graphics in the terminals.

I don't want to fly in a hamburger stand and I do want to have a pouch for my own book if I feel like it. I don't mind the idea of a "no-frills" airline in principle, but then this idea of no frills can be taken too far. It raises the real question, after my personal rant of a one-time bad experience is over and forgotten, of who is responsible for our culture, anyway? Why does "no-frills" have to equate to the worst definition of cheap? And is this just another example of the hideous underbelly of the consumer society? We are attracted to a cheap deal, get gradually used to paying more for less (when we started out by wanting the opposite) and pretty soon forget our values, desires, and to a certain degree, "standards", with the result that we then spawn new generations of consumers who expect nothing, get it, and pay for it, as long as it is "cheap". By that time, everything actually has become cheap in the worst meaning of the word, and it is not so easy to recover or rebuild new values, where service and quality are not matters of price but of maintaining a level of civilization of which any human being ought to be proud.

An argument can be made that, for the sake of a good life on Earth, a reasonable standard of quality ought be maintained in all things regardless of price. This would mean a different way of thinking about, for example, low-cost housing, food and maybe airplane travel. If features have to be cut back or services simplified, at least a "cool factor" (that elusive feeling of a smart, well-produced level of culture and expectation) should be present, so that all users customers are satisfied and feel a part of something really great, not a crass strategy of "value removed". Then the challenge is to provide this at the right price. Surely we are smart enough to figure that out.

I like little restaurants where the food is good and the prices reasonable. I like simple, well-designed products that work well, look good and last for a long time. I prefer smaller cars with style and comfort and simplicity. And I don't mind economy travel when it is inexpensive (like I said at the beginning—few of us can resist a good deal), but I object very much when things are "cheap". The inherent idealism of flying in the sky demands a little more respect!

"Cheap" has no place in culture or civilization and ought not to have the role in economics that it so obviously has. Someone has to have some responsibility for what we produce, and that someone is "us". Consumerism has made us lazy. Good effort needs it's rewards, but are we so complacent and stupid that we measure our achievement with money alone?

Yes, flights are delayed, people make mistakes and life isn't perfect. But there is no excuse for life to be cheap.


*[Speech at the Cumulus Design Education Conference in Utrecht, The Netherlands, 2004]*

# OFF WITH HIS HEAD!

*No es facil ser un hombre sin cabeza, pero lo recomiendo, al menos por algun tiempo. Y eso es parte de la historia que les quiero contar al final de esta charla.*

"The Queen had only one way of settling all difficulties, great or small. 'Off with his head!' she said, without even looking round." Yes, it's not easy to be a man without a head.

For one thing, you can't SEE your own head. It's much easier to see your own feet. But who am I who is looking?

I am a person with a certain identity, culture and heritage from a long line of ancestors I obviously resemble, at least recognizable in some human design features!

I can be traced on a map to countries far away, in Eastern Europe. But I was not born there.

For some strange reason, or a certain human strategy, I emerged on Earth at a different and unexpected location, some thousands of kilometers away to the West. Here is where I was born... in Hollywood!

Some part of this situation was fate, some part geographic and historical, and some part obviously invisible, imbedded as a code in Eastern European human DNA.

But wait a minute: it turns out that the DNA of the fly is not so different from ours: a double helix whose strands produce a strange little
creature with strange characteristics. For one thing, unlike us, a fly is
comfortable upside down. It knows the three-dimensional world in a
rich way: free to move on axes we're not used to.

We can get closer to this knowledge in a small airplane. Balanced by
gravity, lift, centrifugal and centripetal force, sensitive to torque and velocity, we can turn and dive in the air in a more complex way than when
we are glued to the ground.

Having arrived at the ceiling, the fly is now upside-down. Imagine, however, the problem of getting there. It's only recently that researchers
found that it is an end-over-end flip, in the docking maneuver from
level flight to an inverted stop. How easily a fly crosses physical boundaries that we can't!

Let's call the fly a miniature explorer of N-dimensional space:
Theoretically, in the imagination, the tiny fly has possibilities of existence
that seem infinite. It has many channels open, many possible paths to
follow and the freedom to choose a path.

A fly: A tiny upside-down point in space. At night, when a fly enters
the room where a person is sleeping, it changes the environment of the
person just a little. When the fly sticks to the ceiling, it may end up in
the dreams of the sleeper.

A silent presence can be really annoying. And a fly has another
annoying characteristic of not being very clean. But think of it as a
flying metaphor disguised as a thought. Like a fly, a thought is very
often unclean, unformed and illogical. It buzzes through our heads just
like an insect in flight.

A good teacher, like a fly, has these sticky characteristics, landing upside-
down on the ceiling of the student's room, so to speak. Or on her

shoulder. A reminder. The tiny explorer is a reminder to a student who wants to fly and see the world from above. The fly is small, but very strong. And curious! This little traveler of N-dimensional space seems to have a definite desire for discovery.

For a fly, the ceiling might as well be the floor.

At first inspection, that is. A fly is a speck on the ceiling until you magnify it and observe the extent of its evolution. A fly enters new territory with the knowledge that it may soon be upside-down…and delights in it! We don't generally do that, expecting full dimensional stability, and happy when our feet are on the ground. So you look up at a fly on the ceiling and you see only a tiny dot.

Even from close up, you can't see the little hexagons of its compound eyes.

Look down from 1000 meters above land and a human being will also look like a dot. You can't see the color of someone's eyes, find out if they are men or women, or listen to their thoughts. Of course, all insects become totally invisible from here.

From space, all <u>humans</u> are totally invisible. The eye can resolve large landforms, but the national lines that divide them are erased. There is no homelessness, poverty or unrest. We cannot see political prisoners, a damaged environment or national holidays. There is no architecture or literature….or human creativity. And a very different kind of <u>globalization.</u>

Even under a magnifying glass, where you can see the complex structure of a fly's wing, you cannot see its DNA. *Should we ignore what we cannot see with the unaided eye?* What good is an eye that can't see everything? What good is a head that cannot <u>think</u> everything?

In true N-dimensional space, no parameter can be ignored, even when its value is zero. That is to say, a locked door is still, in fact, a door. Like mixing paint, each drop of pure color contributes a component which can be detected in the final pigment. Education and design are like that too. Very multi-dimensional.

When a student asks a question, what dimensions of the answer do you give? What dimensions do you even know? What do you see? We talk so easily about cost, materials, theory, form, function and styling, but what about experience, connotation, resourcefulness and social conscience. It is when a design is infused with a lot of interrelated dimensions that it is most successful. We smile, knowing intuitively, then, that it is good. A design of many dimensions is satisfying, full of subtlety....full of feeling and imagination. These elements are part of the richness of life. Without them, what's the point of design?

Design is arguably a complicated task, involving diverse participants and touching many regions of human emotion and intellect. As such, we owe it to ourselves to contribute in some way to these riches. And to enjoy them as well. That's the job of education somehow, for students and teachers. How we do that is a matter of choice. But ignorance of all kinds of creative opportunities seems at the very least to be a big mistake.

So, after all, it is precisely those things about design that seem most prosaic that turn out to be the most wonderful. In a sense, our whole philosophical understanding of things is upside-down. Our heads got us in trouble. That's why I began to think it is sometimes better not to have a head!

And so about ten years ago I ended up as a visiting professor without a head in Slovenia, not knowing anything, but not far from where some of my DNA originated.

Without a head, somehow I managed to have a very interesting life so far, one which resulted in adventures I would not have had if my head stopped me.

Instead, as a stranger in a beautiful city, my imagination went completely wild, as upside-down as "Alice in Wonderland".

For example, one day I found myself walking down a long corridor, whistling some nice song, and turned to look at my shoulder.

I noticed that this shoulder was not mine, but belonged to someone else, a man without a head, a 3D shadow of me, I think, because it kept following me.

At a point in this corridor I came upon a rabbit...
...and fell through a hole into a thick fog in Ljubljana, Slovenia; it was as though the atmosphere, so heavy with water, got tired, leaning on its elbow for a rest. I was walking at a slow pace, past the National Gallery and the American Embassy.

The tower flashed 21:12, 12°C, and the date 21/12 over the city through a temporary hole in the mist. I didn't realize it was the 21$^{st}$ of December.

The next day, a rainbow formed in the sky, appearing to touch down on Ljubljana Castle. The arc extended majestically to the west, igniting the walls of the castle in a full blaze of color against the sky. I had to assume that the other end of this curve terminated at a location of some significance. On the map I plotted a trajectory.

Due west, at a distance of 800 kilometers was Lausanne, Switzerland. Of course!

It was where SHE lived. I was part of her geometry and another sign that I was crazy...or just in love.

And then it happened. I am standing in the exact center of town in front of the statue of the great poet Preseren. Here I can observe his muse on top of his head as if she were mine. As I walk around the square, I become aware of my shoulders, which seem to want to go in a certain direction as if my own head were no longer in control.

I take a few steps and these shoulders follow, shadowing me. I look again and all at once I am sure that a second "me" is trying to detach itself from my movement, only this being has no head. Arriving at my car, I discover that the passenger side is now occupied by a headless person, who of course cannot speak. I take a turn towards the autoroute. I must have a plan to get rid of him.

The road to Soave is serpentine, and, arriving, I was standing directly in sight of the great castle. My shadow stood there as well, and it was a tender moment in which I could feel his longing for his own pair of eyes, if not his own head, to see the glorious architecture.

And then suddenly I ran for the tower, up the winding stair, in a passage so narrow that there was not enough clearance for a man and his shadow, which ought to leave the unfortunate headless one no alternative but to fly in parallel outside the wall. He was waiting for me at the top, for the first time detached from symmetry and for the first time, independently alive! I grabbed his arm and my frustration sent me spinning, face to the sky and screaming for this creature to let go of me.

As I swung he lifted into the air like a kite and I threw him into the sky, into a strange bird-cloud that shadowed the entire landscape. I could suddenly feel the absence of the other self, the headless flying one. I had caught a glimpse of some other world that passed through mine, but now the rest of the drive through the long flatness of northern Italy was as uneventful as the scene at the castle had been dramatic. Maybe, just maybe, he was gone.

I ascended the road to the Grand St. Bernard tunnel and crossed the Swiss border at 11:11. I arrived in front of her apartment and saw the odometer click to 800 kilometers. The moon was reflected in a puddle of water on the road as I walked towards her building.

She was asleep, and I don't have a key. I rang the bell. I watched the lights go on in her apartment and began following her to the elevator in my imagination. She emerged wearing a thick robe and slippers, and padded to the entrance, smiling. She opened the door and came out onto the steps and walked right through me to embrace the headless man who had appeared out of the moonlight.

Well, it turns out that without a head you still have a heart, and a heart can be broken. But I knew of course that the lucky headless man was really me, and the one WITH a head, whoever that was, maybe also me, was my shadow. Normal life, if there is such a thing, works much better when we think of it in the most irrational way. Everything that seems crazy is probably the truth!

If I had a head I would not be here in Buenos Aires in this upside-down world.

If had a head, I would not have designed a strange clock, or wondered so obsessively about time.

Or marveled at nature....

Or made a prototype on my kitchen table without the proper tools...

or had this crazy clock end up in the catalogue of the permanent collection of the national design museum in New York....

...or gone to Africa.

As a teacher of design, trying to find insight into the process of creativity, I often find myself thinking of design without a head, but with the intuition that comes from the body, or from somewhere else. When we were children we didn't have heads, we just played. And now we're not so sure what we're doing, how to play, what to say.

Without a head, we get scared. So what do we do? We write reports, make theories, study what others have done, and sacrifice ourselves to business or governments or schools, solicit the ill-considered opinions of people in focus groups in supermarkets trying to give everybody what they think they want. And we contribute to a world of diminished expectations, of mediocrity, as we hide behind the façade of the word: "professional".

Real creativity is a series of headless mistakes, because humans simply are not perfect. That is why they are so interesting, and so beautiful.

Humans are clever and find ways of reacting to problems and paradoxes and opportunities; that is to say, they are creative.

This is something children do very naturally, but it is very difficult for adults, and we call this stupid. We once were creative all the time, until someone said "no".

As it turns out, it may be good to be stupid, or at least quite irrational… and live in the rabbit hole where the world is totally upside-down and yet where everything sort of makes sense.

Some brain-imaging of people evaluating working out puzzles, show that activity in a part of the brain goes up significantly. The more activation is recorded, the greater the motivation or ability to seek and correct errors in the real world, a recent study suggests.
The new research supports what many experimental artists, habitual travelers and other novel seekers have always insisted: at least some of the time, "disorientation leads to creative thinking."

If I had a head, I would not be able to welcome you to Pratt Institute… in New York. I arrived at Pratt as chairman of industrial design just a year ago, and of course I have been wondering about the future of design education here since the first day.

Industrial design earned its role as a profession based on a long history of development of principles and techniques. But the fact is that the world has changed with the emergence of high technology, globalization, branding and sustainability; the old idea of problem solving seems to have turned into applying new technology; and finally we have started to think about the consequences of the work we do. One might say that while students were previously expected to take their place in the profession, now they are expected to take their place in the world. And so the shifting times are less about training the servants of industry, but about joining in a creative force of intelligent, powerful and insightful entrepreneurs who are in a position to work effectively and to develop better ideas for the benefit of people.

Well, that's what Plato would have said if he were here. Very logical, and I suppose it's correct. But in a curriculum meeting recently I asked where the metaphor and the heart and the almost child-like wonder of designing was. And spontaneously I realized that the normal process is wrong. It needs to be turned upside-down. The vision is simple: start at the end! With the results. With final projects. And then work backwards.

Keeping in mind that conventional art-based skills may not be the only effective starting point, we know from many examples that giving students room to experiment, develop personal projects, and essentially "build their dreams" may be crucial. Otherwise, skills are not linked to anything the students really care about. Projects tap very fundamentally into the impulse for creativity, even "crazy" experiments, and therefore, right from the very beginning, we should use projects (generated by both students and faculty) to galvanize a process of experimental industrial design education that will continue, even as technologies, ideation media, and processes come and go. Skills come later, as they are needed: the right tool at the right time!

Our heads tell us that we have a responsibility to train designers to get jobs. But in so doing we are seriously underestimating the intelligence of young people, asking them to leave their ideas at the door while they practice conventional skills for a couple of years. Design can wait, we explain.

But if we tell students that they must bring with them a book of crazy project ideas when they arrive at school and then put them directly into an experimental studio, a kind of laboratory for making mistakes and learning from them, guided by the best professors and visiting designers, we have the potential to challenge the students to really investigate their ideas. Students will discuss, write, make rough models and sketches with their mentors, and explore philosophy and theory, materials and methods, presentation and marketing, business and packaging, sustainability and ethics, intellectual property and the Internet, learning how ideas are translated into form in the world. And they will do it all in an integrated studio environment, not in separate classrooms.

Part of making this work is a new sort of student-teacher contract of mutual responsibilities: Currently, students are selected for their promise as designers, hungry for design nourishment, but passive and nagging, like baby birds, mouths wide open, waiting for food from a parent. Teachers are prepared to supply this nourishment every semester, without variation, the same amount to each student in a fixed educational "ritual". Instead, students need to bring their own enthusiasm as well as their own expanding personal book of projects, and of course their curiosity. They must be active participants in the process, experimenting, "failing early". Teachers, on the other hand, agree to tailor their expertise to each student's own needs, with flexibility and willingness to explore ideas together and advance each student's projects.

It's just an idea at this stage at Pratt. The administrative "heads" are wondering what to do with this, but some are excited about the possibility of a small group of students starting an experiment with this program. If we can't do this in school, then where can we do it? It's part of our academic responsibility, but also our academic pleasure: to create a future with adventurous colleagues and students.

So maybe it is not so bad to "lose our heads". Without a head, we would be missing a lot of course: No eyes, but we already see too much. And no mouth, what a pity, since sometimes we say too little. In the end, however, take away all the design, all the theories, all the objects we make and the machines - and what we have left is just us and our stories, going about our lives on the planet... together.

I say that the Red Queen in Alice in Wonderland was right: "Off with our heads!" Let's have some fun...

*[Speech at Encuentro Latinoamericano de Diseño, Universidad de Palermo, Buenos Aires, Argentina 2011]*

Steve Diskin earned his BA in Visual Studies and Masters in Architecture at Harvard University. He began his professional career as an architect with the firm of Kenzo Tange in Tokyo and then with the design of the HELIX clock (now in the permanent collection of National Design Museum in New York). His dual background in industrial design and architecture complemented his 13-year tenure at Art Center College of Design in Pasadena, where he was professor and co-director of the masters program in industrial design. He has lectured extensively at a number of institutions, notably in Argentina, Switzerland, Germany, France, Norway, Denmark, Estonia, Poland and Turkey. Steve Diskin was a Visiting Professor at the Academy of Art, Architecture and Design (VSUP) in Prague and also held a similar position at the University of Ljubljana, Academy of Fine Art and Design (ALUO). In April 2008, Steve Diskin completed his PhD in Architecture at the Ecole Polytechnique Fédérale de Lausanne in Switzerland with his dissertation on technology and urban design. From 2010-2014, he was chairman of industrial design at Pratt Institute in New York.

www.ingramcontent.com/pod-product-compliance
Lightning Source LLC
Chambersburg PA
CBHW020241290526
45784CB00003B/1067